Children at work

Children at work

Edited by Elías Mendelievich

International Labour Office   Geneva

ISBN 92-2-102072-X (limp cover)
ISBN 92-2-102165-3 (hard cover)

First published 1979

Printed by Imprimerie Vaudoise, Lausanne, Switzerland

PREFACE

The aim of this book is to look into the problem of child labour in various parts of the world. It is neither over-technical nor exhaustive : its basic purpose is to make the phenomenon known, to analyse its causes and to put forward possible solutions. It has been prepared by the International Labour Office as part of its contribution to the International Year of the Child.

The study, which was begun on the basis of research carried out at the International Labour Office's headquarters in Geneva, was completed by the preparation of a series of national monographs. This work was entrusted to independent investigators in some 15 countries. Ten of these monographs are reproduced in part in the present volume. It will be seen that the various contributions differ both in content and in length, since each author (or group of authors) has discussed the subject in his own way and since more data are available for some countries than for others. These data may throw light on specific national practice as regards child labour, which may not always observe the legal provisions in force. It should be mentioned here that the choice of countries as examples was motivated only by the desire that all the *regions* of the world in which the phenomenon is most marked should be represented, and it should be understood that the problem of child labour is found to some extent in the great majority of countries. It has naturally been impossible for the ILO to verify all the statements made in the monographs, and the responsibility for the opinions expressed therein, which, owing to the viewpoints adopted, could be questioned in some governmental, professional, economic or university circles, lies with their authors and not with the ILO.

One of the main difficulties encountered in preparing this volume, with respect both to the introductory analysis and to the national monographs, was the shortage—and in many cases the total lack—of statistics and other data. Another major difficulty stemmed from the realisation that the problem of child labour, which is generally illegal, could not be solved only through legislation.

Responsibility for compiling the material for the book was entrusted to Elías Mendelievich, an official on the staff of the Working Conditions and Environment Department of the ILO ; he also prepared Part I (Chapters 1 to 7) and the monograph on child labour in Italy.

After an introductory chapter outlining the problem, Chapter 2 deals with international legislation on the subject and with the ILO's work in this area, together with relevant national legislation and its application. Chapter 3 looks into the extent to which child labour occurs in practice, furnishing statistical and other data on the world's children and describing the various types of employment relationship and the sectors of activity in which children commonly work. Chapter 4 is concerned with working conditions and environment, and Chapter 5 examines children's living conditions and the problems of child labour, together with its repercussions on the child's personal and working life at present and in the future. Chapter 6 discusses the problems of education and training, and Chapter 7 puts forward suggestions and recommendations for future action to improve the conditions of work and life of child workers in the short term and to eliminate child labour progressively in the long term. Part II (Chapters 8 to 17) presents some aspects of child labour in ten countries of Africa, Latin America, Asia and southern Europe. In Appendices A, B and C are reproduced the ILO Minimum Age Convention and Recommendation of 1973 and a document summarising the information received from the governments of ILO member States on the implementation of these international instruments in their own countries. Appendix D gives the text of the Declaration made early in 1979 by the Director-General of the ILO concerning the International Year of the Child, and Appendix E contains the resolution concerning the International Year of the Child and the progressive elimination of child labour and transitional measures adopted by the International Labour Conference in June 1979. Appendix F contains short comments on each of the photographs reproduced in the book, and Appendix G gives suggestions for further reading.

CONTENTS

Acknowledgements

The photographs reproduced in this book are credited as follows : Centre international de reportages et d'information culturelle (CIRIC), Geneva (facing p. 14) ; J.-P. Laffont/SYGMA (facing pp. 15 (below), 78, 79, 94, 95, 110, 111 (above), 126 and 127). It has not been possible to ascertain the sources of the photographs facing pp. 31 (below) and 111 (below), but the ILO will, if notified, be pleased to make due acknowledgement in any subsequent edition of this book. The remaining photographs are taken from the ILO Photo Library, Geneva.

The photographs used for the covers of the book are credited as follows : front cover, top row, ILO Photo Library ; second row, J.-P. Laffont/SYGMA ; third row, J.-P. Laffont/SYGMA, and ILO Photo Library ; back cover, J.-P. Laffont/ SYGMA.

PART I

INTRODUCTORY ANALYSIS

INTRODUCTION

1

To a greater or lesser extent, children in every type of human society have always taken part, and still do take part, in those economic activities which are necessary if the group to which they belong is to survive. However, the notion that child labour is a social problem, a phenomenon hindering the harmonious physical and mental development of the child, is a relatively recent development. This interpretation of child labour, and the accompanying idea that the child should be protected against it, came to the fore when paid child labour (that is, the systematic exploitation of children by employers outside the child's family) became common.

In earlier times children used to work within their family circle. Little by little, through almost unconscious observation, association and imitation, they learnt the role they would be called upon to play as adults. During this process of socialisation, of which his "on-the-job" training formed a part, the child grew to physical and intellectual maturity without ill-treatment and virtually without being exploited, and was simultaneously prepared for adult life. Work of this kind was practically free from harmful effects. It can be likened to those present-day tasks which by nature are light, sporadic, interesting, educational and socially useful and which serve to integrate the child in the social life of the group to which he belongs. (In Nigeria, for example, it is looked upon as a part of the traditional education process—see Chapter 14.) Such tasks are often undertaken as holiday jobs by way of recreation. But against these pleasurable occupations should be set other kinds of job : those that are imposed upon the child, that are occasioned by imperative need, that are carried out under conditions of exploitation, that call for greater physical and mental resources than the exploited child possesses—because they are monotonous, strenuous, harmful or unduly prolonged, because they are a source of worry and because they inevitably imply a lack of schooling, relaxation and general well-being. Jobs of this sort are found in both self-employed and wage-earning employment, and often in modern family enterprises too, albeit usually in a less extreme form ; and the very many children who are engaged on them grow up prematurely and

3

sadly, instead of leading a carefree existence with their friends during what should be the happiest days of their lives.

In those Western nations which are today the most economically advanced countries in the world, it was taken for granted in the past that children would work alongside their parents in the fields or in the home. However, when the change-over to manufacturing industry took place neither the institutions nor the legislation of those countries were adequate to meet the changed circumstances. Thus in the nineteenth century it became common for children to work in factories, especially textile mills, from the age of 6 years onwards, in abysmal working conditions involving a daily stint of some 14 hours and with almost no means of protection against the risk of accidents. Even as recently as the beginning of the twentieth century, some Western children were still being employed in coal mines or were kept busy at home on work sent out to them by manufacturers. [1] Happily, in most developed countries economic, moral and legal progress has relegated exploitation of this kind to the past. This is not to say, however, that child labour in these countries, despite its being illegal, has completely disappeared, as we shall see later. In the developing countries and in southern Europe the exploitation of children has not been eliminated and is still prevalent or fairly widespread in many places.

SOCIAL, ECONOMIC AND CULTURAL BACKGROUND

If we are to understand why child labour today takes the forms that it does, the phenomenon must be set against its social background. Broadly speaking, we may say that child labour persists in inverse relation to the degree of economic advancement of a society, country or region. The exploitation of children is one result of the complex, unchanging nature of society, not only in most of the developing countries but also in some regions of the developed world. The notion of child labour is rooted in the traditions and attitudes of the regions where it is practised, as a remnant of the past, a form of resistance to change. As an illustration of this, we may mention the belief, very widely held in the developing countries, that the more children there are in a family, the more hands there are to help to increase the family income. Whether this belief be justified or not, it is merely a tradition, handed down from generation to generation. Again, in the developing countries the idea that a child who is no longer a baby should be maintained without working is uncommon. This idea stems not so much from poverty as from the traditional belief that there is no point in making any plans beyond those for satisfying the family's immediate basic needs. It is an idea that betrays an attitude devoid of any impulse for evolution and change. Following the same train of thought, reference is sometimes made to an age-old educational principle that is based only on the need for survival : that if one does not work one has the option of starving or of stealing. This principle is applied from a very early age. In fact, when the need for survival and the social function of traditional behaviour converge, long-term planning becomes irrelevant : today's meagre incomes, out of which any savings are impossible, cannot be sacrificed in the hope that tomorrow's incomes and other benefits might be greater.

In such a social setting, whenever a child decides or agrees to work in order to earn his living he thinks he is taking the decision himself. The truth of the matter is that this decision has in effect already been taken for him, through the attitude of his parents and through the influence of the entire social environment in which he lives : that is, he accepts a role which turns him into both the victim and the involuntary accomplice of an unjust situation.[2] Once this kind of thinking is accepted, it is clear that the parents who benefit directly or indirectly from the exploitation of their children do not consider that they are deliberately acting in a despotic and inhuman manner ; rather, they believe that they have a natural right to take advantage of (not to exploit) all the family's resources, which generally amount to little more than the number of hands it has at its disposal. Furthermore, the parents consider that, as in the family undertaking of former times, the child is learning a job that will be of value to him in the future, without their being aware of the harmful effects that certain forms of work at an early age can have on the child. It is not the family that should carry the blame for the fact that the child has to work, since the courses of action open to the family are few in number : it is society as a whole that is at fault. Like all social problems, child labour is not an isolated phenomenon, nor can it ever be so.

THE ROLE OF LEGISLATION

Custom and the law usually hold that the work that children do alongside their parents is distinct from the exploitation to which they may be subjected when they work for third parties. Indeed, this is generally so, since parents usually look after their children's welfare ; nevertheless, however much the physical effort, the hours of work and the boredom inflicted on the child may be reduced and however satisfactory his working environment may be, he will inevitably be concerned in the smooth running of the family undertaking and will inevitably share, with his parents, problems, preoccupations and uncertainties which are not usually the concern of children of his age.

It was in the more developed countries that people first became aware of the harmfulness of child labour and of the need to introduce compulsory education and to give children the necessary opportunities for recreation, and legal and practical measures were gradually introduced to this end. It does seem, however, as though these measures were not always inspired purely by humanitarian motives. They were also designed to protect the employment and wages of adult workers.[3] In fact, it is known that children who enter the labour force carry out work that could very well be done by an adult—that is, they usually deprive an adult of the job in question. Moreover, the child does the job for a much lower wage than would have to be paid to an adult. For this reason many employers prefer to engage children, knowing that they can pay them lower wages than if the same type of job were to go to an adult. There is in fact a vicious circle here : on the one hand, child labour increases unemployment among adults and reduces their income ; [4] and on the other, the unemployment and low wages of adults force them to put their children to work in order to boost the family income. Thus child labour simultaneously increases and reduces the family income ; but, as is clear, it reduces rather than increases that income.

In the developing countries, however, it has unfortunately not been possible to put an end to child labour (despite the fact that almost all these countries have good legislation in this respect)—neither to protect children from exploitation nor to safeguard the employment of adults. As we have seen, in these countries it is often taken for granted that children have to work, and it is considered perfectly normal that they should be paid low wages for doing so. Children therefore usually play a relatively important productive role within their respective families. This is true both in the towns and in the country. The tasks that they have to carry out (whether in place of the adults of their own family, whom they have displaced on the labour market, or jointly with them) represent an appreciable economic income (that is, appreciable in relation to the low level of the family income). Within this distorted economic framework, and because of the lack or insufficiency of social security, the working child finds that it is he who has to support his old, ill or unemployed parents.

If, on the one hand, child labour is prohibited by law in virtually all countries, on the other hand the numerous human societies in which children do in fact work can neither provide all the children with direct or indirect means of subsistence from other sources, nor make available to them the educational and cultural facilities and the means of recreation that they so badly need. In such circumstances families cannot avoid having to send their children illegally to work, and employers will continue to engage them illicitly. Thus for large numbers of children there are only two alternatives : either to go to work (which would mean that the law was being broken) or to sink into enforced idleness in an environment which offers comparatively few opportunities of going to school and in which recreational facilities are lacking, with the result that the child is tempted to drift into vagrancy, if not outright delinquency. Those who have to work during their childhood years have no chance of going to school and of obtaining qualifications which might help them to escape from their state of poverty. Inevitably, when their extreme destitution obliges them to look for an immediate source of livelihood, their lack of qualifications keeps them in low-paid, unqualified jobs—the usual vicious circle, once again.

For the very reason that the work that the children do is illegal, the law makes no provision for safeguarding their working conditions. Children thus constitute a labour force outside the law, and consequently do not enjoy the right to claim the social benefits that should be due to them. In other words, children make up a submissive and defenceless labour force with no possibility of negotiating their conditions of work (which are usually imposed unilaterally and arbitrarily by the employer), with no trade union to defend them and with virtually no access to sickness or employment injury insurance or social security schemes (where such exist). A good number of these problems also affect children who work legally—that is, those who work in countries were the minimum age for admission to employment is fixed by law at a very low level (12 or 13 years). The great social advances secured by adult workers do not in fact apply to working children, who are exploited as if those advances had never been won.

As children who undertake an adult's job do not possess the physical and mental capacity that these jobs call for, their work is usually done less efficiently than if it were performed by an adult ; if, in fact, the employer benefits economically from such work, it is rather because he pays very much less for it than because it is done efficiently.

The most recent ILO standards on the matter fix the minimum age for admission to employment at 15 years and recommend, with various provisos, that this be gradually raised to 16 years. [5] However, at the national level the minimum age has been fixed by law at anything from 12 to 16 years, depending on the country. In other words, in some countries children who work from the age of 12 or 13 years are not breaking the law. Their work is not clandestine and no legal objection can be made against it. However, when we recall that the ILO standards have been drawn up for clear-cut humanitarian reasons, it seems evident that all these countries should bring their own standards into line with the ILO standards and that all work carried out by children who have not reached the age laid down in those standards is harmful, whatever may be the legal minimum age for employment in their own countries. In the meantime, those countries where the legal minimum age is very low should introduce vigorous and practical measures to guarantee that the children concerned benefit from special protection. We may mention here, by way of example, that in some countries where the production of hand-made carpets is a particularly important industry the minimum age for employment is very low ; at the same time, it is common knowledge that large numbers of children work in this industry specifically because they have small and nimble fingers, as well as for all the other reasons underlying child labour that we have already mentioned. Needless to say, in these countries the legal minimum age, which is already much lower than that laid down in the ILO standard, is often not respected.

CHILD LABOUR IN PRACTICE

In the developing dual economy countries, children can be found working both in the modern sector (or in contact with it) and in the poor sector to which they belong. The social status of these children, however, is always low, coming as they do from the poorest classes of society.

The proportion of children in the total labour force of an undertaking varies from one extreme to the other. In some undertakings they make up a small minority, in others they are fairly numerous, and in others again they make up almost the whole of the labour force. The proportion depends in fact on the country (which has its own customs and traditions in the matter), on the kind of undertaking, on the relative difficulty of the work, on the availability of child labour, on the degree to which children can adapt themselves to the tasks that are asked of them, and so on.

Clearly, the more children he employs, the more an employer can reduce his production costs ; at the same time he increases his share of the value added produced by the work of the child, whose own share is correspondingly lower.

The exploitation of children who work is tacitly accepted by all as a component of the social framework. It is, however, often difficult to decide whether an employer is taking advantage of child labour because the child in question is living in poverty and has no alternative but to let himself be exploited, or if, through pity, he wishes to help to alleviate the child's poverty through an activity that has become an integral part of the social scene.

THE REASONS WHY CHILDREN WORK

Within this social framework in which a centuries-old tradition impels the child to work from an early age, the most pressing reason for him to seek work is the need to reduce to the greatest extent possible the poverty in which he is living and thus to help him to satisfy his basic needs. Even the smallest payments in cash or in kind are welcome in the poverty-stricken home in which, as a rule, he lives. Moreover, the child is led to believe that he must work from an early age through solidarity with the family group, so as to compensate as much as possible for the economic burden that he represents and to share in the maintenance of his family, which is usually a very large one. Today, very many children in the developing countries consider it quite normal that they should continue the family tradition of not attending school and of beginning work at a tender age, irrespective of the degree of poverty of the family. Another reason why children work is the parents' wish to keep their children occupied and off the streets, so that they do not get up to mischief, that is, be tempted to drift into vagrancy with all its consequences. Of course, this argument is valid only when the child finds a job indoors and cannot be put forward when he is sent to work on the streets in the first place.

Children may also feel obliged to work because they are doing badly at school and because there is no other alternative. If the parents are able to let the child go to school for only a few years, it is likely that he will encounter more difficulties during his years at school than a child from a better-off family. However, in many cases the parents prefer to send the child out to work rather than to school, either because there is no school within a reasonable distance of the family home, or because they cannot do without the income the working child brings in, or because they cannot meet the costs of sending the child to school, or again because they cannot see what use schooling would be to him.

Another direct cause of child employment is the situation at home. There may be tension and uncertainty, provoked or increased by poverty ; the father may have left home ; the mother may be alone ; the father or the mother, or both, may fall ill, or become physically unfit, or die. However, the argument that the children are obliged to work because of the disappearance of the breadwinner is often fallacious, because it is generally the head of the family himself who sees to it that his children go out to work.

Again, when a rural family migrates to the town, the adults are straightaway faced with a new and unknown environmental and labour situation. As a result of the instability and insecurity that this causes, the children are often set to work so that the family may survive.

In the developing countries the driving force behind every case of child labour is, of course, poverty ; but the basic cause is usually a combination of some of the factors that have just been mentioned. A study recently undertaken in Bangkok among several hundred working children revealed that the principal reasons they gave to explain why they were at work were as follows (two or more of the reasons, or even all of them, may evidently have been put forward by the same child) : [6]

Reason given	Percentage
Poverty	23.4
Need to assist parents in household economic activity	32.9
Parents want them to work	26.3
Need to earn their own living	7.9
Better than doing nothing	6.9
Other reasons	2.6

In general, children take up a particular job for one of the following reasons :

(a) it is the only type of job open at the time they are looking for work (this may well involve a hasty choice which can affect their whole future life) ;

(b) one or more members of the family are already doing that kind of job ; and

(c) the work in question does not call for any special qualifications (which means that the children will certainly remain at a very low vocational level).

At any rate, the most important need for impoverished families is to earn some money in order to live ; other, not strictly vital needs will be satisfied only as and when possible. It is true, however, that many very poor children are inveigled by the publicity media into obtaining objects and services that are proclaimed to be the symbols of well-being. Thus, what the media claim to be necessities become more important than the real basic needs—that is, those to do with physical development, health, affection and culture. Psychologists explain that this craving for the superficial and superfluous is a reaction against a feeling of deprivation and even of frustration.

In the developing countries today, and within the limits of the opportunities open to them, children who spend their time at work do at least keep clear of delinquency, begging, the marginal subcultures of the street and other similar evils.

In the developed countries the picture is completely different, since in those countries children do not work in order to meet their basic needs or because they are following tradition but in order to earn a little extra money, and the parents do not put pressure on their children to get a paid job during the years when they should legally be going to school. Moreover, far fewer children go out to work, and if they do, the work is in any case done outside school hours.

By far the greater number of working children in the less developed regions hand over their entire earnings to their parents or to the relatives with whom they are living ; or else the parents or relatives receive the money direct from the child's employer, the aim as always being to increase the family's total income. After the payment has been made, most parents who are in a position to do so give a little money to the child who has earned it. This is usually spent on something to eat, or on a cinema ticket or school equipment, clothes and, where possible, a bicycle. Some children give their parents only about half their earnings, in line with the local custom, and keep the rest for themselves.

In these regions there is practically no entertainment within the reach of working children. In fact, there is a general lack of recreational activities, playing fields, parks, premises for the healthy use of spare time, cultural associations, and so on. Spare time is usually given over to resting, playing simple games or sometimes going to the cinema. For want of recreational activities, the child is often simply bored during his spare time, and the boredom can lead to vagrancy. However, the child who is exploited never has spare time enough to think of playing or of amusing himself—not to mention those children who work and study at the same time.

Notes

[1] See Lela B. Costin: *Child welfare: Policies and practice* (New York, McGraw-Hill, 1972).

[2] M. Luisa Piccione: "La piaga del lavoro minorile", in *Formazione Domani* (Rome), Nov.-Dec. 1974, p. 49.

[3] Martin Hamburger: "Protection from participation as deprivation of rights", in *New Generation* (New York), Summer 1971, p. 2.

[4] Armando Cocco: "Lavoro minorile apprendistato scuola", in *Formazione Domani,* Jan. 1975, p. 51.

[5] See Chapter 2 and Appendices A to C.

[6] Office of the Prime Minister, National Statistical Office: *Children and Youth Survey, Thailand, 1975* (Bangkok).

THE LEGISLATIVE FRAMEWORK

2

STANDARD-SETTING ACTIVITY OF THE ILO
AS REGARDS MINIMUM AGE FOR ADMISSION
TO EMPLOYMENT

Since its foundation in 1919 the ILO has been much concerned with the gradual elimination of child labour and the promotion of the well-being of children in the fields within its competence. [1] Indeed, in the Preamble to the Constitution of the ILO it is stated, inter alia, that "conditions of labour exist involving such injustice, hardship and privation to large numbers of people as to produce unrest so great that the peace and harmony of the world are imperilled" and that "an improvement of those conditions is urgently required" in many domains, including the protection of children and young persons. [2] In the Declaration of Philadelphia the International Labour Conference, meeting in 1944, recognised the solemn obligation of the ILO to further among the nations of the world programmes which, among other things, would achieve provision for child welfare. [3]

At the very first session of the International Labour Conference, which was held in the year of the ILO's foundation, a Convention was adopted which fixed the minimum age for admission of children to industrial employment at 14 years. At subsequent sessions of the International Labour Conference various Conventions and Recommendations were adopted on the minimum age for admission to employment in different sectors of economic activity. Thus between 1919 and 1965 10 Conventions on this subject were adopted. Finally, in 1973, the Convention concerning Minimum Age for Admission to Employment (No. 138), together with the corresponding Recommendation (No. 146), were adopted. These two instruments are reproduced in Appendices A and B. As can be seen from the text of Convention No. 138, this Convention replaced all the previous relevant Conventions, that is, its purpose was to establish minimum standards valid for all sectors of economic activity.

There is no doubt but that these international standards have done a good deal towards stamping out many of the abuses that are caused by the exploitation of children. However, much remains to be done if national legislation and practice throughout the world are to be brought in line with the provisions of Convention No. 138 and of Recommendation No. 146.

During the heated debates that took place at the 53rd Session of the International Labour Conference in 1973, when this Convention was adopted, some delegates maintained that it was unrealistic to fix the minimum age for admission to employment at 15 years in the developing countries, since to do so would be to disregard the social and economic conditions prevailing in those countries at the present time. It was also claimed that if the Convention fixed standards that were too high for the developing countries, they could not be enforced and would remain a dead letter. The idea was also put forward that it would be much better to proceed by stages, since for the time being the period of compulsory schooling (where and when it had been introduced) ended before a child reached 15 years of age, and that, in any case, the children of the Third World countries should be able to work before that age so that they might contribute to the maintenance of their families. These arguments were unacceptable to those who supported the raising of the minimum age, who maintained that the point at issue was to eliminate the exploitation of cheap child labour.

Convention No. 138 lays down, inter alia, that with a view to ensuring the effective abolition of child labour, the minimum age for admission to employment should be raised to a level consistent with the fullest physical and mental development of young persons. This age should not be less than the age of completion of compulsory schooling and, in any case, should not be less than 15 years. The Convention nevertheless admits the possibility that in those member States whose economy and educational facilities are insufficiently developed the minimum age may be fixed at 14 years. In any case, any member State which has ratified the Convention can subsequently notify the ILO that the minimum age originally laid down has been raised. Moreover, a member State whose economy and administrative facilities are insufficiently developed may initially limit the scope of application of the Convention and similarly may extend that scope at a later date. However, the provisions of the Convention must be applicable as a minimum to the following : mining and quarrying ; manufacturing ; construction ; electricity, gas and water ; sanitary services ; transport, storage and communications ; and plantations and other agricultural undertakings mainly producing for commercial purposes, but excluding family and small-scale holdings producing for local consumption and not regularly employing hired workers. The Convention further provides that national laws or regulations may permit the employment or work of persons 13 to 15 years of age on light work, on condition that such work is not likely to be harmful to their health or development, nor to prejudice their attendance at school or their participation in vocational orientation or training programmes. These two conditions also apply to work in general carried out by persons who are at least 15 years of age but who have not yet completed their compulsory schooling. However, a member State which, in line with the provisions mentioned above, has fixed the minimum age for admission to employment in general at 14 years, may, as long as it continues to avail itself of these provisions, permit young people of

12-14 years to undertake light work and young persons who are at least 14 years of age but have not yet completed their compulsory schooling to undertake work in general, still in the light of the provisions that were mentioned above in relation to young people of 13-15 and 15 years respectively. As regards work which is likely to jeopardise the health, safety or morals of young persons, the Convention lays down that the minimum age for admission to any type of employment or work of this kind shall not be less than 18 years ; however, notwithstanding this provision, member States may fix this age at 16 years, on condition that the health, safety and morals of the young persons concerned are fully protected and that they have received adequate specific instruction or vocational training in the branch of activity concerned.

In order to make it easier to apply the principles laid down in Convention No. 138, Recommendation No. 146 advocates, inter alia, a firm national commitment to full employment; the progressive extension of other economic and social measures to alleviate poverty, thus making it unnecessary to have recourse to child labour ; the development and progressive extension of social security and other family welfare measures, including children's allowances ; the development and progressive extension of adequate facilities for education and vocational orientation and training; the adoption of special measures as regards children and young persons who do not have families or who do not live with their own families and also of migrant children and young persons ; and the introduction of compulsory full-time attendance at school or participation in vocational orientation or training programmes, at least until the age of admission to employment laid down in Convention No. 138. The Recommendation also proposes that member States should take as their objective the progressive raising to 16 years of the minimum age for admission to employment.

At its 204th Session in November 1977 the Governing Body of the ILO considered that the ILO's contribution to the International Year of the Child should include a special effort to promote the implementation of these two new standards on the minimum age for admission to employment. Accordingly, it decided to invite the governments of member States (a) to consider taking such further action as might be necessary to give effect to the provisions of Convention No. 138 and Recommendation No. 146, and to consider the ratification of that Convention if they had not already ratified it ; and (b) to inform the Director-General of the ILO before 31 July 1978 of any such action taken or contemplated and of any difficulties which in their view stood in the way of the implementation of the instruments in question and the ratification of the Convention. The results of this inquiry are reproduced in Appendix C.

Other steps recently taken by the ILO on the occasion of the International Year of the Child and in order to strengthen its activities concerning the protection of working children and the gradual elimination of child labour through legal, educational, social and economic measures include the

Declaration by the Director-General of the ILO concerning the International Year of the Child (endorsed by the Governing Body at its 209th Session in February-March 1979) and the Resolution concerning the International Year of the Child and the progressive elimination of child labour and transitional measures, adopted by the International Labour Conference in June 1979. These two texts are reproduced in Appendices D and E respectively.

RELEVANT NATIONAL LEGISLATION AND ITS APPLICATION

Legislation

Practically every country in the world has adopted legislation on the minimum age for admission to employment. The setting by law of a minimum age below which young people are not allowed to work is done with the intention of preserving their physical and mental health and their moral welfare and at the same time of making it possible for them to go to school. Indeed, in many countries, especially the most industrialised nations and the socialist States (irrespective of their level of development), compulsory schooling is a factor which tends to limit child labour since the end of compulsory schooling is generally set at 14, 15 or 16 years, depending on the country.

The absolute legal minimum age for admission to employment varies between 12 and 16 years from country to country, but in each country there are exceptions to the general rule, as we shall see below. In some countries children are allowed to work at a lower age than the normal when they are engaged on non-industrial jobs or on light tasks. On the other hand, in dangerous or harmful occupations the minimum age is usually fixed at a higher level. In many countries the legislation on the minimum age for employment does not cover those working in domestic service.

Among the examples of national practice that could be given we may cite the following.

In the Byelorussian SSR, Czechoslovakia, France, Norway, Romania, the Ukrainian SSR and the United Kingdom the general minimum age for employment is 16 years. [4]

In Japan children are not allowed to work until they reach the age of 15 years ; this age corresponds to the end of compulsory schooling. However, the employment of children is allowed from 12 years of age, outside school hours, in certain specific light jobs that are not harmful to their health and welfare.

In India there is no general provision in this respect ; the minimum age for employment may be from 12 to 15 years, depending on the sector of activity.

In Senegal children are forbidden by law to work before they reach the age of 14 years, but the law permits those of 12 to 14 years to carry out domestic jobs or light and seasonal tasks if the father or guardian agrees.

In Argentina too, work below the age of 14 years is forbidden, but an exception is made for those between the ages of 12 and 14 years in family undertakings or, provided that permission is granted by the competent authority, when it is considered that the work is indispensable if the child is to support himself.

In the United Kingdom the general prohibition mentioned above is relaxed in the case of part-time work and work carried out during the school holidays. Such jobs may be undertaken by youngsters of from 13 to 16 years of age. According to the Government of the United Kingdom this concession does not infringe the provisions of Convention No. 138 as regards light work. Children are forbidden to work on the public highway below the age of 17 years.

In a few countries children are allowed to work from the age of 12 years, but the legislation which makes this possible contains specific protective clauses. In Morocco, for example, the minimum age of 12 years applies to all kinds of jobs, including those in agricultural work, but employment in dangerous jobs is forbidden to persons less than 16 years old.

By far the largest number of children who work—both in the developed and in the developing countries—do so in agriculture. In about 50 countries agriculture is in principle covered by the same minimum-age provisions as industry and in a score of other countries by provisions setting a lower minimum age. But in many States the relevant provisions are very limited in scope, or apply to only part of the agricultural sector, or else they exclude it altogether. [5]

Application

The degree to which the minimum-age legislation is applied varies widely by country and sector of activity. We may say, for example, that this legislation is generally observed in the undertakings in the modern sector of the economically developed countries. In the modern sector of the economically less developed regions the legislation is fairly well applied, with variations between one country and another. In agriculture—and particularly in small family agricultural undertakings—a tremendous number of children are kept hard at work, and thus the national laws or regulations, where these exist, are broken or children work without legal protection. Without asking ourselves why something is considered to be against the law in one country and not in another, we must recognise that, for obvious reasons, it is practically impossible to apply laws and regulations on the prohibition of child labour in agriculture in the less developed regions. Furthermore, it is in any case practically impossible to supervise their application.

The same difficulties of application are found in the wage-earning sector in agriculture and also in the various combinations of wage-earning and non-wage-earning activities found in rural areas.

In both the agricultural and the urban sectors the fact that children who work in family undertakings are either excluded altogether from the coverage of the relevant legislation or derive only piece-meal benefit therefrom is a very serious handicap. The law-makers must of course have had very sound reasons for allowing these exceptions ; however, the fact that they did not attack the phenomenon in the very sector in which it is the most widespread does considerably reduce the effect of any legislative measure aiming at the over-all protection of working children.

In the economically less developed regions there is one sector in which enormous numbers of children work. This is the so-called informal sector. Virtually none of the legal provisions relating to the minimum age for employment and to the protection of children in general are observed in this sector, and relationships between employers and workers are usually governed not by legislation but by tradition and custom. In fact, a very large number of employers and workers in this sector are quite unaware of the existence of the relevant legislation.

In conclusion we may say that modern legislation, which was created in response to the needs of a specific socio-economic situation and was well adapted to meet those needs, is ill adapted to the conditions prevailing in vast areas of many countries. At this point several questions may be asked about the extent to which the legal prohibition of work below a specific age can be applied in these sectors. How, for example, can its influence be effectively brought to bear on the present situation ? What concrete measures can be taken to protect working children when the relevant legislation is inadequately applied? How can the necessary structural changes be put in hand?[6] The truth of the matter is that in many countries the legal provisions aiming at prohibiting child labour (as well as many other provisions which it is not our task to analyse here) are seen as an ideal, as an objective for the future—but, in view of the actual situation in large parts of the country, not as standard-setting provisions which can be immediately and rigidly enforced.

Perhaps because they are conscious of this imbalance between the ideal and the true situation, the general public take child labour for granted, without thinking overmuch about it, although they are well aware that children are employed in the service industries or in street trades and that the relevant legislation is virtually powerless to deal with the situation. Even the authorities themselves usually close their eyes to this nominally illegal phenomenon and accord it a wide measure of tolerance. There is a very widespread feeling, among both the authorities and the general public, that if the law is no longer to be broken in this way things will get worse rather than better—that is, where poverty is rife, to take the child away from his work and to eliminate exploitation will not lead to his enjoying a happier life. The crux of the matter is that either he works, to the detriment of his physical and mental well-being, or else he faces starvation.

Labour inspection

The visits which labour inspectors make to undertakings may be either routine or special. Special visits are carried out in particular circumstances, from 1975 show that, out of a total world population of 3,968 million souls, informs the competent authorities that the standards in force are being infringed. If the labour inspectors find that the legal requirements relative to the prohibition of child labour are not being observed in an undertaking they have visited, they must explain the legislation to the employer, demand that the employment of the young person or persons working there be ended and possibly penalise the employer in the manner laid down by the law.

In some countries, such as Hong Kong and Italy, the labour inspection authorities have become alarmed in recent years by the large numbers of children working illegally. Inspection campaigns have been organised for the sole purpose of detecting this specific type of infringement of labour law. In both countries the inspectors were able to unearth very many cases where the law was being broken and to impose the relevant legal sanctions. In Hong Kong, with its small area and its very high degree of industrialisation, the results obtained seem to have been so encouraging that the authorities hope to be able to stamp out child labour completely by 1979, while at the same time introducing various social welfare measures for children. In Italy, on the other hand, the measures taken have succeeded in revealing the size of the problem but so far do not seem to have contributed greatly towards solving it (see Chapter 12).

In Indonesia labour inspectors visited 800 undertakings in six provinces during 1976, as part of an inquiry into child labour and the conditions under which it is carried out. The inspectors came up against two main difficulties in their task : locating the undertakings which employ children, since these undertakings are not officially registered ; and ascertaining the exact age of the children working (see Chapter 11). The inspectors eventually succeeded in establishing the following points :

(a) children are employed in a wide variety of jobs in handicrafts, in the food, building, textile, cigarette and soap-making industries, in labelling, cleaning bottles, transporting and stacking bricks, cleaning floors, and so on and so forth ;

(b) children may be employed either with or without a labour contract. In the latter case they help workers (usually parents or other members of the family) who are bona fide employees working on a piece-rate basis. Whether or not children are engaged as workers in a factory depends on the type of job ;

(c) most of the children have received some education or are still going to school. In Central Java, East Java and North Sulawesi, respectively, 65 per cent, 57 per cent and 20 per cent of the children have never been to school at all ;

(d) the wages received by the children vary from region to region. They can range from 25 rupiah per day for cigarette cutting in Central Java to 350 rupiah in North Sumatra. Some 60 to 70 per cent of the children usually receive between 75 and 100 rupiah per day (the exchange rate at the time of writing is US$1 = 415 rupiah) ;

(e) none of the undertakings provide for health insurance or for any other kind of social security ;

(f) with a few exceptions children work only during the hours of daylight (that is, between 6 a.m. and 6 p.m.) and the total number of working hours does not usually exceed seven per day and 40 per week. Children will occasionally work overtime if the other employees are doing so. However, in North Sulawesi children employed in the sea-fishery industry work an average of three hours per day between 1 a.m. and 6 a.m. ;

(g) in Central Java, East Java and North Sulawesi only, the age of the children working is estimated to be in some cases less than 10 years. The great majority of the children employed are estimated to be between 12 and 14 years old ; and

(h) none of the 800 undertakings visited has an in-plant vocational training or general education programme.

In those countries where recourse is had to child labour on a large scale and in which the attitude of the labour inspectors towards the employment of children is strict, the employers teach the children the art of deception, in case the inspectors pay the undertaking a surprise visit. For example, an employer might maintain that a child who was actually working for him was in fact a relative or a friend of the family who was just passing through or who had come to deliver a message ; other employers have installed hiding places or rush the children off the premises through the back door or a window. In other countries labour inspectors show a good deal of tolerance when they come across children working, believing that this phenomenon is a necessary evil, and limit themselves to checking their working conditions and environment, with the aim of improving hygiene, safety and lighting, reducing the hours of work, and so on.

In agriculture, which as we have seen is the very sector where child labour is most widespread, especially in the less developed regions, labour inspection is practically non-existent. The reasons for this are obvious : there would have to be many more inspectors, who would have to travel enormous distances every day, at enormous expense, in order to bring to light a relatively small number of infringements.

The shortage of staff and needed equipment is also the reason why it is quite impossible for labour inspectors to visit the tremendous number of small undertakings in the informal sector.

Notes

[1] ILO : *Minimum age for admission to employment,* Report IV(1), International Labour Conference, 57th Session, Geneva, 1972, p. 3.

[2] *Constitution of the International Labour Organisation* (Geneva, ILO, 1977), p. 5.

[3] ibid., pp. 24-25.

[4] See Appendix C, para. 21.

[5] ILO : *Minimum age for admission to employment,* op. cit., p. 17.

[6] See Chapter 7.

CHILD LABOUR IN PRACTICE

3

SOME DATA ON POPULATION

The inevitable result of the population explosion that occurred in most countries, especially those of the Third World, during the 1950s and 1960s was a considerable increase in the number of young people. Figures dating from 1975 show that, out of a total world population of 3,968 million souls, 1,428 million, or 36 per cent, were less than 15 years old. The proportion in the developed regions was 25 per cent (1,132 million and 283 million respectively), as against 40.4 per cent in the developing regions (2,836 million and 1,145 million respectively (see table 1). In many developing countries children less than 15 years of age make up between 40 and 50 per cent of the total population, although in a few the proportion is nearer that which is commonly found in Europe, as for example in Argentina where it is about 29 per cent. [1] If, however, we leave aside these few developing countries where the lower percentages are found, it is apparent everywhere in the Third World that the presence of such a large number of young people causes tremendous social and labour problems. What is to be done, for instance, about their upkeep, their employment, their wages ?

Statistics on child workers

We have already seen that in the developing countries there is a traditional tendency to place children in jobs that could well be done by adults. This pressure by young people on the adult labour market is increased by the very fact that there are so many of them. The figures given in table 1 are revealing in this respect.

The ILO estimates that at the time of writing, in the world as a whole, 52 million children aged less than 15 years are working. By far the majority of these are unpaid family workers, as table 2 shows. Moreover, this figure of 52 million may well be an underestimate, since in some countries young workers less than 15 years old are not included in the labour force statistics. In others young people who both work and go to school are rarely considered as being part of the labour force. Again, the statistics cover only those

Table 1. Total and economically active population by sex and age-group (mid-year 1975) (Thousands)

Area and age-group	Males			Females			Total		
	Total population	Economically active population Number	Per cent	Total population	Economically active population Number	Per cent	Total population	Economically active population Number	Per cent
World									
−15	727 757	32 630	4.5	700 428	22 086	3.2	1 428 185	54 717	3.8
15–19	199 893	111 018	55.5	192 389	70 953	36.9	392 282	181 972	46.4
20–24	176 661	152 268	86.2	171 322	87 800	51.3	347 983	240 069	69.0
25–44	497 162	479 573	96.5	484 253	246 286	50.9	981 415	725 859	74.0
45–54	173 396	163 753	94.4	177 004	91 330	51.6	350 400	255 083	72.8
55–64	114 679	92 868	81.0	126 084	42 031	33.3	240 764	134 899	56.0
65 +	97 600	37 759	38.7	129 425	15 218	11.8	227 026	52 977	23.3
Total	1 987 149	1 069 870	53.8	1 980 905	575 705	29.1	3 968 054	1 645 575	41.5
More developed regions									
−15	144 468	972	0.7	138 563	577	0.4	283 031	1 549	0.5
15–19	50 377	22 603	44.9	48 466	18 374	37.9	98 843	40 976	41.5
20–24	47 775	40 206	84.2	46 337	30 721	66.3	94 111	70 927	75.4
25–44	152 301	147 394	96.8	152 148	90 870	59.7	304 449	238 264	78.3
45–54	63 039	59 140	93.8	71 449	43 147	60.4	134 488	102 287	76.1
55–64	43 082	32 425	75.3	55 188	15 759	31.8	98 271	50 003	50.9
65 +	46 295	10 627	22.9	72 196	5 449	7.5	118 491	16 076	13.6
Total	547 337	313 366	57.3	584 348	206 715	35.4	1 131 684	520 082	46.0

Less developed regions

− 15	583 289	31 658	5.4	561 865	21 509	3.8	1 145 153	53 168	4.6
15-19	149 516	88 416	59.1	143 923	52 580	36.5	293 439	140 995	48.0
20-24	128 886	112 062	86.9	124 985	57 080	45.7	253 872	169 142	66.6
25-44	344 861	332 179	96.3	332 105	155 416	46.8	676 966	487 595	72.0
45-54	110 357	104 613	94.8	105 555	48 183	45.6	215 912	152 796	70.8
55-64	71 597	60 443	84.4	70 896	24 453	34.5	142 493	84 896	59.6
65 +	51 305	27 132	52.9	57 229	9 769	17.1	108 535	36 901	34.0
Total	1 439 812	756 504	52.5	1 396 558	368 989	26.4	2 836 370	1 125 493	39.7

Africa

− 15	88 965	6 087	6.8	88 354	3 555	4.0	177 319	9 641	5.4
15-19	20 865	13 748	65.9	20 655	7 335	35.5	41 519	21 083	50.8
20-24	17 373	15 589	89.7	17 438	7 262	41.6	34 811	22 852	65.6
25-44	45 406	44 199	97.3	46 975	20 425	43.5	92 381	64 624	69.9
45-54	13 005	12 539	96.4	13 623	6 179	45.4	26 628	18 718	70.3
55-64	8 089	7 262	89.8	8 795	3 316	37.7	16 884	10 579	62.7
65 +	5 428	3 353	61.8	6 534	1 292	19.8	11 962	4 645	38.8
Total	199 130	102 777	51.6	202 374	49 366	24.4	401 504	152 142	37.9

Latin America

− 15	69 016	2 447	3.5	67 215	831	1.2	136 231	3 278	2.4
15-19	17 337	9 690	55.9	17 017	3 947	23.2	34 354	13 637	39.7
20-24	14 543	12 699	87.3	14 428	4 617	32.0	28 971	17 316	59.8
25-44	36 526	35 109	96.1	36 814	9 182	24.9	73 340	44 292	60.4
45-54	11 566	10 745	92.9	11 764	2 507	21.3	23 329	13 252	56.8
55-64	7 509	5 963	79.4	7 905	1 194	15.1	15 415	7 157	46.4
65 +	5 722	2 615	45.7	6 730	475	7.1	12 452	3 090	24.8
Total	162 220	79 269	48.9	161 872	22 753	14.1	324 092	102 022	31.5

Area and age-group	Males			Females			Total		
	Total population	Economically active population		Total population	Economically active population		Total population	Economically active population	
		Number	Per cent		Number	Per cent		Number	Per cent
Northern America									
−15	30 794	253	0.8	29 572	125	0.4	60 366	378	0.6
15-19	11 831	5 308	44.9	11 419	3 982	34.9	23 251	9 290	40.0
20-24	10 874	9 128	83.9	10 639	6 207	58.3	21 513	15 335	71.3
25-44	29 667	28 299	95.4	30 202	14 812	49.0	59 870	43 111	72.0
45-54	12 545	11 655	92.9	13 472	7 720	57.3	26 017	19 375	74.5
55-64	10 203	8 207	80.4	11 540	4 946	42.9	21 742	13 153	60.5
65 +	9 919	2 375	23.9	14 165	1 218	8.6	24 084	3 593	14.9
Total	115 832	65 224	56.3	121 010	39 010	32.2	236 841	104 234	44.0
Asia									
−15	444 234	23 281	5.2	424 490	17 171	4.0	868 724	40 453	4.7
15-19	116 936	67 186	57.5	111 690	43 002	38.5	228 626	110 187	48.2
20-24	103 008	88 780	86.2	99 065	49 085	49.5	202 073	137 864	68.2
25-44	285 532	275 011	96.3	271 059	137 259	50.6	556 591	412 269	74.1
45-54	93 892	89 127	94.9	88 910	44 425	50.0	182 801	133 552	73.1
55-64	61 307	51 634	84.2	60 549	22 577	37.3	121 857	74 211	60.9
65 +	45 169	23 376	51.8	50 332	8 947	17.8	95 501	32 324	33.8
Total	1 150 079	618 394	53.8	1 106 094	322 466	29.1	2 256 173	940 859	41.7
Europe									
−15	57 831	477	0.8	55 261	341	0.6	113 093	817	0.7
15-19	19 174	9 607	50.1	18 375	8 036	43.7	37 549	17 643	47.0

20-24	18 555	15 717	84.7	17 896	11 185	62.5	36 451	26 902	73.8
25-44	63 819	61 803	96.8	62 201	31 479	50.6	126 020	93 282	74.0
45-54	27 899	26 264	94.1	30 194	14 929	49.4	58 093	41 193	70.9
55-64	19 801	15 204	76.8	23 779	7 502	31.5	43 581	22 706	52.1
65 +	23 548	5 109	21.7	34 764	2 652	7.6	58 313	7 761	13.3
Total	230 628	134 181	58.2	242 470	76 124	31.4	473 098	210 305	44.4

Oceania

− 15	3 431	86	2.5	3 272	64	1.9	6 703	149	2.2
15-19	1 029	591	57.4	973	501	51.5	2 002	1 092	54.5
20-24	946	860	90.9	885	514	58.0	1 832	1 374	75.0
25-44	2 780	2 691	96.8	2 590	1 141	44.1	5 370	3 832	71.4
45-54	1 114	1 060	95.1	1 055	453	42.9	2 170	1 513	69.7
55-64	817	683	83.7	838	211	25.2	1 655	894	54.0
65 +	694	176	25.4	882	46	5.2	1 576	222	14.1
Total	10 812	6 147	56.8	10 496	2 929	27.9	21 308	9 076	42.6

USSR

− 15	33 846	—	0.0	32 263	—	0.0	65 749	—	0.0
15-19	12 720	4 888	38.4	12 261	4 150	33.8	24 981	9 039	36.2
20-24	11 362	9 495	83.6	10 971	8 930	81.4	22 333	18 426	82.5
25-44	33 431	32 462	97.1	34 413	31 987	92.9	67 844	64 449	95.0
45-54	13 376	12 363	92.4	17 987	15 118	84.0	31 362	27 481	87.6
55-64	6 953	3 915	56.3	12 677	2 284	18.0	19 630	6 199	31.6
65 +	7 120	755	10.6	16 018	588	3.7	23 138	1 343	5.8
Total	118 448	63 878	53.9	136 589	63 058	46.2	255 038	126 935	49.8

Source. ILO : *Year Book of Labour Statistics 1978* (Geneva, 1978), pp. 16-47.

Table 2. Number of working children less than 15 years old

Area	Total (millions)	Unpaid family workers [1]	
		Millions	Percentage of total
World	*52.0*	*41.2*	*80*
South-east Asia	29.0	23.2	80
East Asia	9.1	6.4	70
Africa	9.7	9.2	95
Latin America	3.1	2.0	65
Europe	0.7	0.4	50
USSR	—	—	—
North America	0.3	—	10
Oceania	0.1	0.1	85

[1] Includes a very small number of persons working on their own account.
Source. ILO, Bureau of Statistics and Special Studies.

youngsters who have a fixed job, and thus exclude the majority of those who work only occasionally. In short, it is impossible to make an accurate estimate of the numbers employed, for the simple reason that, since in most countries child labour is clandestine, it is in the interest of all the parties concerned to conceal it.

We can therefore see why estimates of the extent of child labour should vary so widely in different countries. In Italy, for example, the most favourable estimates put the figure at a maximum of some 100,000, on the grounds that there is a marked decline in child labour throughout southern Europe. The ILO *Year Book of Labour Statistics* for 1978 gives a figure of 114,000. Yet some estimates that have appeared in the press recently maintain that the figure is nearer to half a million, and maybe much higher. In Spain it has been suggested in various periodicals that there could be some 200,000 children at work, whereas the *Year Book* gives 142,000 only.

In the developed countries generally, thanks to legislation, compulsory schooling, tradition and the economic situation, the number of working children is very low. The only exceptions here are children who work in agriculture, a certain number of street traders and delivery boys (especially of newspapers) and those who work in family undertakings.

USUAL AGE AT WHICH WORK IS BEGUN

The age at which children usually begin work depends on tradition, the size of the undertaking and whether or not it is a family concern.

In some countries parents set their children to work on household chores, in the fields or on other family tasks when they are still at a very early stage of physical development. Again, children may be apprenticed to a craft when they are very young indeed—sometimes no more than 6 or 7 years old (see Chapters 8, 10 and 16). Of course, the higher the age-group, the greater the proportion of children in that age-group who go out to work ; thus, most working children are between 13 and 15 years of age. In general, the intensity and the duration of the work they perform also increases as the years go by, not only because the children gradually become stronger and more skilful but also because they spend less time playing games and going to school (if they do so in the first place). The age at which domestic servants are hired ("adopted" is perhaps the more exact word, as we shall see later) usually varies between 9 and 10 years.

In some countries a child may be illegally declared to be older than he really is, so that on the face of it his employment situation seems to be in order.

In many cities in all regions of the world a large number of children aged between 11 and 13 begin their working life delivering newspapers, doing their round every morning before going to school.

An inquiry[2] carried out among some child workers in India revealed the following points : 24.7 per cent of the children had begun work between the age of 6 and 9 years ; 48.4 per cent between 10 and 12 years ; and 26.9 per cent between 13 and 15 years. The results of another inquiry, [3] carried out a few years ago in Portugal by the Portuguese Industrial Association among 19,040 adult workers in 230 mechanical engineering undertakings, showed that 3.6 per cent of the women had begun their working life between the ages of 5 and 7 years, that 10.3 per cent of them had done so between the ages of 8 and 10 and that the proportion for those who had begun to work between the ages of 11 and 13 was 41.1 per cent. In other words, 55 per cent of the women in this survey had started work before they had reached the legal minimum age for admission to employment.

SELF-EMPLOYMENT AND DIFFERENT TYPES
OF EMPLOYMENT RELATIONSHIP

Many young people work for themselves, usually by providing street services or by peddling goods for sale. However, a good proportion of the children engaged in these activities are not self-employed but work for third parties (who may or may not be members of their own family), either for a fixed payment or for a percentage of the monies they earn or receive from sales. These two types of payment are also found in the more stable jobs : for example, when the child is a genuine wage earner ; when he is apprenticed to a craft but has no contract ; and when he collaborates with an adult worker from outside his family (in agriculture, a factory or a home industry) and has no direct relationship with the adult worker's employer. When the child works within the family circle (generally without payment) he may be a member of a small handicrafts undertaking, a group of peasant small-holders, a landless farming family working for a third party or a family group working at home for a third party. The children who work in some shops and stores have no contact, either direct or indirect, with the owners, who simply agree to their presence as packers or errand boys, and it is the customers themselves who tip the children for their services.

SECTORS IN WHICH CHILDREN WORK

In which sectors of economic activity are children usually employed when they go to work? Several factors have a bearing on this question—economic needs, tradition, the relative speed of modernisation, the rate of population increase, rural-rural and rural-urban migration (seasonal or more or less permanent), whether the country or region is predominantly rural or urban and/or industrialised, whether the society in which the child lives is a tribal one, and so forth.

Developed countries

In the more developed countries the overwhelming majority of children who work do so in agriculture, in family or non-family undertakings, during the school holidays and outside school hours, but above all at harvest and sowing time, on a wide range of jobs which may at times be heavy and dangerous. The minority who work in urban centres are employed in the sales or distribution sector (delivering papers, milk, etc.), in hotels and restaurants, [4] especially in holiday resorts and during the school holidays, and in some light and occasional jobs such as baby-sitting.

Developing countries

In the developing countries child labour is most common in agriculture, [5] in services (provided for the most part on the street) and, as a last resort, in industry. Those who are wage earners generally work in the informal sector, usually in small undertakings that are often not registered as such and that hence do not observe the legal requirements as regards taxes, social security, safety and health, and so on. The larger, registered undertakings in the modern sector, which comply with all legal and other requirements, obviously do not usually employ children—rather than run the unnecessary risk of falling foul of the labour inspectorate, they prefer to have recourse to the large reserves of non-qualified or semi-qualified adult manpower (see Chapter 14).

In agriculture children are accustomed from an early age to working with their parents, either on the family plot or for a third party. When they

work on the family holding they begin by carrying out light tasks such as looking after animals, collecting firewood and fodder and drawing water ; later they learn to sow and to reap. In commercial agriculture in very many developing countries children commonly form part of the work team composed of the whole family ; they are kept busy on jobs such as weeding, spreading fertiliser and tending plants, but often they share in the heavy work done by the adults—ploughing, sowing and reaping. In southern Europe they are frequently employed individually as labourers on large farms. In particular, it has been reported that in almost all regions of the world the plucking of the coffee bean is a job largely done by women workers helped by their children. [6]

In many developing countries entire families will move from one farming area to another, following the cycle of agricultural work ; however, when the head of the family goes off alone to work for a few seasons as a day labourer on someone else's estate, the wife and children of these small farmers look after the family plot in his absence.

Following the rapid urbanisation of the past few decades, child labour in the cities has greatly increased. The child who arrives in the city on his own accepts the first job that he is offered, in order to survive. In reality the job opportunities in the disadvantaged urban zones are fewer than back home in the countryside, and only a few of the young migrants manage to earn a little money. In the big cities there are more opportunities for children to work in the services and handicrafts sectors than in small towns and, especially, rural areas.

Many of those who work on the streets begin by helping their father (usually without payment). Subsequently they might strike out on their own or continue to work for their father or for a third party. The jobs they do are very varied : cleaning shoes, guarding parked cars, loading and unloading goods, carrying messages, selling magazines, food, sweets, flowers, lottery tickets and so on, collecting junk and other goods, and so forth. In certain specified areas in both developed and developing countries young people are involved in drug-running or prostitution, in which many of the girls exploited by adult organisations begin their economic activity at the age of 12. Finally, on the streets in the less developed countries one can see many children begging on their own account or exploited ; and it has been reported that they are sometimes deliberately maimed by their own parents.

Many children provide various kinds of service in small workshops and commercial establishments, acting as assistants, messengers, packers, carwashers, mechanics, panel beaters, cleaners, petrol-pump attendants, waiters, bellboys, chambermaids, barbers, and so on. A large number of children are also employed in domestic service.

In manufacturing and handicrafts undertakings in the developing countries children are, relatively speaking, fewer in number. They are nevertheless very active, both in family and in non-family undertakings or doing jobs on their own account in their own homes. In many factories they do not participate directly in production operations but carry out tasks such as packing, glueing and labelling. In other undertakings they are in fact engaged in production jobs—for example, in bakeries, in matchworks, in the food industries, in the textile industry (winding, carding, spinning, weaving, etc.), in the tailoring and leather industries (cutting, sewing, embroidering), in metal, leather and woodwork shops, in pottery shops (firing, modelling, painting), in undertakings making shoes, toys, fireworks, and so forth. In cigarette factories, especially in south and south-east Asia, children clean and cut the tobacco and roll the cigarettes. In many countries, over a vast area stretching from north-west Africa to south Asia, children are an important source of labour for the traditional carpet-manufacturing industry. In south and south-east Asia they are also employed in glassworks. In some countries they work in the building industry, especially in the informal sector : usually (though not always) they carry out light tasks such as carrying materials or cleaning up. In some countries children of 10 or 11 years old can be found in almost all industries performing the same jobs as adults. [7]

SECTORS RESERVED FOR BOYS OR FOR GIRLS

In many regions and social groups tradition dictates which jobs should be done by boys and which by girls. It often happens that boys are preferred because they are stronger, because they produce more and because they are less exposed to the dangers of the street and other workplaces. For example, in agriculture, in those regions where tradition allows the employment of both sexes, the heavier tasks (ploughing, weeding, sowing and reaping) are generally reserved for boys, while the girls busy themselves in milking, cooking, sewing, looking after their younger brothers and sisters, and so on.

As regards work on the public highway, the situation can vary greatly, depending on local tradition : either the boys alone provide services or engage in selling, so that the girls are not exposed to the hazards of the street ; or the boys perform certain services and sell certain goods, with others being performed or sold by the girls. For example, boys can often be seen selling newspapers and cleaning shoes whilst the girls sell food.

In general, family undertakings employ children of both sexes, depending on the nature of the jobs to be done and the type of business.

In some countries or regions certain jobs are not thought worthy to be done by children of one or the other sex. In others a combination of tradition and conservatism ensures that boys are employed much more than girls, especially within certain social classes, or when there is a desire to emulate the standards of those classes. In some circles it is not considered "honourable" that a girl or a woman should contribute economically to the running of the household and the practice of sending girls to work outside the home is frowned upon. For women not to have to work outside the home is a sign of a higher social status. In various countries, regions and social and cultural milieux, marriage is the sole or principal purpose in life for the woman, and to this end the girl needs only to learn how to do domestic tasks. This tradition is, however, changing more or less rapidly, depending on the region, and the proportion of girls who work seems generally to be on the increase. Where there exists a marked sexual discrimination regarding the jobs that girls can do, it is justified by arguments such as : girls are only interested in and capable of jobs that are traditionally or typically women's jobs and that are compatible with their future life as housewives ; girls should not, and in any case have no desire to, work in industry and services because these sectors call for skills and knowledge that are more masculine in nature ; boys should show interest only in jobs that call for strength, skill, greater knowledge, etc. These beliefs go back many centuries, during which the economic roles of the sexes were based on their degree of physical strength, and a major cause of the present trend towards a levelling of the differences seems to be the reduced importance of this physical strength and the increased importance of skill, intelligence and the use of tools.

If there is a strong resistance to female child labour in some regions and social milieux, in others the fact that the boys are looked upon as being the more important members of the family means that a greater effort is made to send them to school, whereas the lot of the girls—who "have no need of book learning"—is to work. This practice is usually more widespread in rural than in urban areas : the girls work on the family farm or do paid seasonal work. This is why in schools in these areas there may be many more boy pupils than girl pupils.

Finally, in some countries and sectors differences of sex have no influence on the jobs undertaken : thus, in some handicrafts workshops in some countries (for example, Thailand—see Chapter 17), boys and girls are employed on the sole criterion of personal ability.

Notes

[1] See Chapter 8.

[2] M. Singh, V. D. Kaura and S. A. Khan : *Working children in Bombay : A study* (New Delhi, National Institute of Public Co-operation and Child Development, 1978), p. 90.

[3] "O trabalho dos menores", in *Infância e Juventude* (Lisbon), Jan.-Mar. 1973, p. 17.

[4] "Work out of school : The Emrys Davies Report", in *Education* (London), 10 Nov. 1972.

[5] See, for example, Chapters 8 and 15 ; and Mostafa H. Nagi : "Child labor in rural Egypt", in *Rural Sociology* (Urbana, Ill.), Dec. 1972, pp. 623-627.

[6] ILO : *Conditions of work of women and young workers on plantations,* Report III, Committee on Work on Plantations, Sixth Session, Geneva, 1970, p. 24.

[7] For further information concerning the sectors in which children work, see ILO : *Minimum age for admission to employment,* op. cit., Ch. III.

WORKING CONDITIONS AND ENVIRONMENT

4

GENERAL CONSIDERATIONS

In the developing countries the children in families which have their own undertakings are introduced to work gradually by their parents. However, other parents, together with relatives or family friends, often get in touch with possible future employers in order to "place" a child in a job at a later date. Usually the first employers to be approached in this way are those for whom the parents, relatives, friends or neighbours work themselves. When a child takes up a job on the street, here too it is often the parents or relatives who first push him into it. In some countries employers who need a child to work as an unqualified assistant (for example, in a pastry shop or a dairy) look for and engage one in a small rural town. Female domestic servants usually come from rural areas : often they get in touch themselves with the families for whom they are going to work, but in other cases their parents hand them over to their future employers so that they can be "adopted" as a subordinate member of the household. [1] This is virtually tantamount to selling the child or giving her away. In parts of Africa, Latin America, Asia and southern Europe it is not unknown for parents to hand over their children at the age of 8 or 9 years, so that they may work as farm labourers or shepherd boys, in return for which the parents usually receive a small loan or payment in cash or in kind. (Needless to say, this practice is a flagrant breach of the law.) In this way many needy parents forgo the custody of their children and the exercise of parental authority. There have been reports that in south and south-east Asia some employers take possession of a number of children, against their will, and exploit them ruthlessly (see Chapter 15). The newspapers in the countries concerned sometimes bring to light cases of the exploitation of young people—inhuman conditions of work in factories, shepherd boys being sold, children being given away, and so on.

In these regions, when a child is dependent on the employer in this way, it is the employer himself who, in the vast majority of cases, fixes the child's general conditions of work, arbitrarily and unilaterally. As a result the treatment that the employer metes out to his dependent young workers varies widely and depends on his character, on the mood he is in and on local customs. Thus the working child may find that he is greatly imposed upon and severely treated, with neither respect or consideration. Ill-treatment may include corporal punishment, abuses of all kinds, humiliation and frustration. The possibilities for exploitation are, in practice, unlimited. Other employers may be paternalistic, protective and generous. Between these two extremes the general tendency is for the child to be treated rather badly since, as we have seen, he has no way of defending himself.

If children were allowed to work in the formal sector, their general conditions of work would be much better ; but because they are legally prohibited from doing so (and in the formal sector this prohibition seems to be respected), instead of not working at all they are generally thrown back on to the informal sector, where general conditions of work are usually appalling and where welfare facilities are conspicuous by their absence (see Chapters 12 and 13).

Many children who are claimed by the employers to be apprentices do in fact learn very little about the job in which they are supposed to be qualifying ; more often than not they are kept busy running errands or carrying out disagreeable or difficult tasks which often have little connection with the job to which in theory they are apprenticed, or are treated as servants and receive little or no remuneration. The lucky ones, however, do serve some sort of apprenticeship, despite the poor conditions under which they work.

Notwithstanding these manifestly bad working conditions, many child workers seem to be satisfied with the pay and benefits they receive, with their hours of work, with their working environment and with the attitude of their employer and older fellow-workers, as well as with the treatment they receive. The reasons behind this feeling of job satisfaction probably lie in the low level of their job expectations and in the fact that they are receiving some small income and are not unemployed.

The tasks on which they are engaged are generally monotonous and repetitive in nature ; occasionally, they are light but often they are ill suited to the child's physical and mental capabilities.

There is no doubt but that it is in urban areas that child workers are treated the worst, exploited the most and undergo the greatest privations, especially in manufacturing industry. Very frequently they have to work under difficult conditions, as for example in stifling heat in a restricted space or, if in the open air, without being able to shelter from the rain or keep out of the sun. They may be forced to work in an awkward position in badly lit, badly ventilated, noisy or unhealthy premises, in damp and unhygienic surroundings, in an atmosphere contaminated with dust or gases, inhaling tobacco dust, crammed together with other workers, without adequate means of security, without special resting areas, without medical facilities, without water for washing, without adequate toilet facilities, and so on and so forth. It is not unusual for them to have to lift and carry heavy loads, in violation of the principles laid down in the relevant ILO standards (see, for instance, Chapter 12).

Although the number of women in domestic service is tending to decrease in most countries, it is common knowledge that in many cases domestic servants are exploited with no consideration being shown to them, and sometimes are even ill treated. In most of the countries where domestic service is widespread, the difference in social status between the employer and the employee is such that the former may adopt a somewhat contemptuous attitude towards the latter, even when he is paternistically inclined towards her.

Although many self-employed workers work in their own homes, others have to travel varying distances, on foot, by bus or by train, to reach their workplace, just as many wage earners do. Children who are more or less self-employed, and child street traders generally, feel that they are freer than children who work in other sectors. Some are exploited only a little, others not at all, and some enjoy the protection of their parents. Many of them, however, despite their relative freedom, are exploited by their parents or relatives as well as by adults outside the family circle. When carrying out their activities they are hardly ever protected from the vagaries of the weather ; if they do not operate from a fixed location they are molested by the police or by groups of youths or adults, and if they do have a fixed location this does not usually meet even the most elementary conditions of hygiene nor does it have toilet facilities.

Normally, the child who works in a family undertaking, be it in agriculture, manufacturing, commerce or handicrafts, is exploited less than the wage-earning child. Indeed, the stress, fatigue and harmful effects to which he is exposed are partly compensated for by the personal attention and affection which his parents can give him, during both work and rest periods.

A recent study observes that in one country the children of farm workers who migrate to another part of the country work in conditions that recall the exploitation to which in earlier times the children of the Western world were exposed in the factories and mines. Their plight is aggravated by the educational problems they have to face. [2]

HOURS OF WORK ⌐

In the developing regions there seems to be more employment instability among working children than among adults. This reflects the general instability that is characteristic of those in the younger age-groups, of whom it may be said that the more they are under the control of their parents or employers, the less they are likely to change jobs ; but when the initiative lies in their own hands, the poor working conditions, low wages and ill-treatment which are their lot give them ample reasons for doing so.

The length of time that wage-earning children work each day and over the year varies considerably according to their availability for work (i.e. whether they go to school or not and/or whether they have other jobs as well), the parents' wish to keep them at work more or less continuously, how long the employer needs them, and so on.

The child who is self-employed can vary his working hours according to his own capabilities and needs, although, if he is to ensure that his activities are to be profitable as possible, he must take account of the times when his potential customers are at their most numerous and adjust his working hours accordingly : for example, a child selling newspapers or food must be at his site very early in the morning when the newspapers are published, and again during the rush hour, when the cinemas empty, during market hours, and so on. Even so, it is not unusual to find 8- or 9-year-old children outside the big hotels of a Third World metropolis at 11.30 at night, still trying to sell the morning edition of the daily newspaper.

Many youngsters work only during the school holidays, at weekends, early in the morning or late at night. Temporary jobs are common in the construction industry (usually in the informal sector) and in public works : here the youngsters work for as long as the job for which they were taken on lasts, or for that part of the job for which child labour was foreseen. Seasonal work in the tourist industry, especially in the services sector, is also often undertaken by children ; agricultural work too needs many young people and children for seasonal tasks such as sowing and harvesting.

The number of hours worked by children each day varies considerably. They may be at their jobs every working day but for part of the day only, or they may work eight hours a day for six days a week, and so on. Since, as we have seen, the general conditions of work are generally fixed by the employer alone, all kinds of abuses are encountered : working days of 10, 12 or 14 hours for six or sometimes seven days a week, that is to say far beyond what the child can tolerate both physically and mentally. [3] Sometimes children do not work strict hours at all—they merely stay on in the shop or café where they work until the last customer has left.

To gain an idea of the length of time that many child workers spend away from home, one must of course add to the number of hours worked the time for work breaks and for travelling to and from home.

As has already been mentioned, in some countries girls work longer hours than boys, because boys spend more time at school. Two studies carried out in Indonesia (Java) and Nepal recently produced the details shown in table 3 on the daily hours of work for children of both sexes.

For both self-employed and wage-earning children the working week seems generally to be excessively long, with six or even seven days per week being worked in various sectors of activity. It is common knowledge that girls in domestic service usually work very long hours, since they must be available at virtually any time to carry out their employer's bidding.

At certain times of the year in specific localities in the developed countries there is a great and urgent need for child labour. At sowing and harvest times and in the high summer season many children work an excessive number of hours per day on seasonal jobs. In these countries the number

Table 3.   Indonesia (Java) and Nepal : daily hours worked by children

Country and age-group	Hours worked per day	
	Boys	Girls
Indonesia (Java)		
6-8	3.6	3.5
9-11	3.3	5.4
12-14	4.8	8.7
Nepal		
6-8	3.7	4.9
9-11	6.5	8.4
12-14	7.5	9.9

Source. M. Nag, R. C. Peet and B. White : "Economic value of children in two peasant societies", in International Union for the Scientific Study of Population : *International Population Conference, Mexico, 1977* (Liège, 1978), Vol. 1, tables 1-4.

of hours worked by the minority of children who do some part-time job during the school term is usually not related to the socio-economic status of their families. [4]

Some wage-earning children are permitted to take work breaks at fixed intervals during the working day. Others are not allowed to do so, however —despite the fact that a child needs a break more often than an adult, if he is to recharge his physical and mental batteries. It will be readily understood that, in the case of a girl in domestic service, her work breaks (and indeed her conditions of employment generally) depend purely on her employer's wishes : she may have the right to rest after lunch, or again she may not ; and it can happen that she has to work for six, seven or even more hours at a stretch.

The period of daily rest is often insufficient, especially in agricultural work, industry, some service industries and domestic service.

The weekly rest is sometimes granted and paid, sometimes granted but not paid and sometimes not allowed at all—that is, the working week is a seven-day week.

In many countries and undertakings young wage earners do not enjoy the annual paid holidays that are laid down by law for adult workers carrying out the same job. Nor do young people working at home enjoy annual paid holidays.

REMUNERATION

In the less developed regions especially, children who work in the family undertaking usually receive no payment for their work, since the family income is considered to be one indivisible whole. This is equally true when the family carries out agricultural work for a third party : the children take part in the work and the head of the family receives the total sum earned.

When the child is a wage earner, his wages are usually derisory in relation to the value of the work he produces, and are in any case much lower than those received by an adult doing the same job—perhaps only a half or a third (or even less) of what the adult worker earns, according to the criterion applied by the employer (see Chapters 12 and 13, for example). To justify this criterion the employer put forward various reasons, depending on the case : the child worker has not had enough experience, and so his work cannot be well done ; he has no family responsibilities ; training him costs the employer money, which he has to recover by paying the child less. . . .

In Chapter 15 there is a very typical example of this : the workers suggested to the employers that, as in this particular case the children were clearly doing the same work as the adults, the children should be paid the same wage as the older workers. This suggestion was not accepted.

A still more flagrant example is that of the supposed apprentices who are in fact working rather than learning, and are not being paid for it. Such a state of affairs may sometimes last for years. Even in countries where the legal age for admission to employment is 12 years, young people of that age are often not paid the legal minimum salary. When they work overtime they are generally paid at the normal rate (which is already unfairly reduced). When the child does not work directly for the employer but with an adult worker, the latter usually pays the child a share of what he has earned.

With regard to payment for piece-work, the child is at a clear disadvantage here as compared with adult workers, since, for obvious reasons, he usually produces less than they (or is more tired, or both).

Some child workers are paid a fixed wage plus tips. Others live by tips alone, and under such a system there can of course be no regular source of income. Takings can vary greatly, according to circumstances, and offer no guarantee of a basic minimum wage.

In general, the income of child street traders is irregular, for many reasons : location of their pitch, time of the month, times when the streets are crowded, nature of the goods offered for sale in relation to the taste and purchasing power of the potential buyers, percentage of the takings the child retains if he is working for a third party, and so on.

In commercial agricultural undertakings there are children whose wages are extremely modest (when in fact they are not merely housed and fed). In some kinds of commercial and industrial undertakings it is customary for part of the wages to be paid in cash and part in kind. For many parents the fact that a child is housed and fed outside the home, even though he contributes nothing to the family budget, at least takes part of the pressure off it.

OCCUPATIONAL RISKS

To a greater or lesser extent, the risk of occupational accidents or diseases is present in every employment sector. The risk that child workers run in this respect is heightened in that their bodies are not so strong as those of adult workers. During his day's work, and depending on the job he is doing, a child experiences fatigue, faces one or more potential accident situations, adopts uncomfortable positions which give him aches and pains, and often works in dirty conditions, with all the dangers of infection that this implies.

The self-employed child who has an accident or contracts a disease of occupational origin obviously benefits from no form of social protection. If the child is a wage earner he is not usually protected either, since in the vast majority of cases he is working illegally, as we have seen. If he is the victim of an occupational accident or disease, he and his parents must be prepared for fearful and irreversible consequences. For obvious reasons, the official statistics reveal only a very small proportion of the occupational accidents and diseases that affect young people.

Agriculture is one of the most hazardous sectors for the physical safety and health of workers, for several reasons : the prevalence of dangerous modern machinery ; prolonged exposure to heat, sunlight, dust, wind and insects ; the almost constant physical effort that agricultural work demands ; contact with various chemical products, such as fertilisers and pesticides, whose long-term effects on man may be completely unknown and for the majority of which, in cases of poisoning, no specific antidotes exist. Children are particularly at risk from endemic and parasitic diseases, diseases of the respiratory tract, dermatosis and fatal accidents.

In industry the unhealthy conditions have a greater impact on the safety and health of child workers than on that of adults, because of their want of experience in handling tools, because of that lack of concentration which is quite normal for their age and because of a shortage of security and prevention equipment such as masks and special gloves. For example, in glass-works children suffer greatly from the suffocating heat and run the risk, amongst others, of sustaining cuts and burns (see Chapter 17). Children employed in carpet manufacturing breathe wool dust throughout the working day, and this penetrates deep into their lungs.

It should also be borne in mind that, as machinery, tools and workplaces in general are designed for use by adults rather than by children, they are a further potential source of more or less serious accidents, and call for increased effort by the child as well as causing numerous problems of adaptation.

Of the countless occupational hazards which can befall children especially, we may mention that in several countries it has been discovered that, after several months of use, a certain glue used in the leather industry can produce paralysis, which affects in particular the more delicate organisms—that is, those of children. In general, solvents (for descaling metal, for example) and glues (in carpentry and the leather industry) are particularly harmful to children because of the toxic vapours that such products give off.

In the construction and public works sectors, even though here children usually carry out light tasks only, they are none the less exposed to a wide variety of potential accidents and other hazards—falls, injuries, consequences of inclement weather, and so on—because on the one hand these are sectors in which accidents are common and on the other hand the immaturity and lack of concentration of children make them more liable to accidents than adults.

Young street traders are exposed, at times until late at night, to the vagaries of the weather, to dirt of all kinds, to traffic hazards, to detention by the police on grounds of vagrancy and to everything that is most sordid in city life. Reflecting on the large numbers of child workers among juvenile delinquents, the authors of an inquiry carried out in the United States in the early years of the present century found that the mere fact of going to work on the streets, rather than bad home influences or lack of schooling, was the major cause of juvenile delinquency. [5]

The problems and dangers inherent in work in commerce, the service industries in general and domestic service are less serious. However, the risks to children of such accidents as falls, injuries and cuts, and the consequences of carrying loads that are too heavy for them, especially in domestic service, need to be borne very much in mind.

Notes

[1] See ILO : *Minimum age for admission to employment,* op. cit., p. 27.

[2] Costin, op. cit., pp. 77-78.

[3] In Bombay it was found that children employed in hotels and restaurants were working an average of 11.61 hours a day (Singh, Kaura and Khan, op. cit., table 67). See also Chapters 12 and 13.

[4] "Work out of school : The Emrys Davies Report", op. cit.

[5] Edward N. Clopper : *Child labor in city streets* (New York, Macmillan, 1912 ; reprinted by Garrett Press, New York, 1970), pp. 159 ff.

LIVING CONDITIONS 5

HUMAN ENVIRONMENT, HOUSING AND HEALTH

In the less developed regions the living conditions of the child worker are generally appalling. Poverty and over-crowding are compounded by squalid housing with noisome sanitary installations, where these exist at all. The abysmal quality of the housing is a widespread social problem, above all in urban areas. Sometimes up to ten members of a family may be crammed together in the shacks and hovels in which they live—often in a single room, with little or no ventilation. Such conditions are typical of any developing country with a high rate of population growth. [1] Chapter 16 illustrates the situation in one such country.

Human relationships under such conditions are frequently not good, and the child does not receive as much affection as he ought. The father is frequently an alcoholic. Inevitably, the child's welfare is affected by living under such conditions. Not enough attention is paid to the young members of the family, nor are they adequately supervised ; consequently, many of them lead a semi-independent life from an early age. The combined incomes of all members of the family rarely make it possible to improve their conditions and quality of life.

In some developing countries with warm climates children who have either been abandoned or who have made their own way from rural areas can be seen wandering about the city streets. As they usually have nowhere to go, they sleep on the pavement. Others who have a job but no home sleep in market stalls or in a corner of the workshop where they work (which can be damp, dirty, unhealthy, full of vermin, and generally unpleasant). Others sleep in the kitchen of the café or bar where they are employed, others again do so surrounded by the scrap metal and junk they have collected during the day, and so on.

Children who work or are looking for work are usually badly clothed and undernourished, especially in urban areas. They generally do not have enough calories, protein, calcium and vitamins. Their diet is usually very poor and unbalanced : in Mexico City, for example, they basically live on *tortillas* (maize cakes), coffee and beans.

The number of children in these regions who suffer from poor health is enormous. Working children are even worse off in this respect. The great majority of them work even when they are ill. Vitamin and protein deficiency, anaemia, bronchitis and tuberculosis are widespread. The onset of tuberculosis, although this is not a typical occupational disease (unlike the others) but one caused by grim living conditions, is encouraged when the child begins to work at a tender age and works long and tiring hours in a harmful work environment.

The child who works on the streets can quickly be led astray into begging, delinquency and other social evils. In an attempt to counteract this trend, homes and centres have been established in some countries for those children who do not want to go back to their own homes, from which they may have run away and where the social atmosphere may be demoralising.

Housing, sanitary conditions and the nutrition and physical development of working children in southern Europe are showing a general improvement over those that obtained in the past.

PERSONAL PROBLEMS OF WORKING CHILDREN

In the less developed regions children who do not work in the family undertaking do not have enough contact with their parents, because they spend the greater part of the day away from home and often come back late in the evening. This is yet another factor contributing to the disorganisation of family life.

When a child begins to earn some money, he has the feeling that he is more important than he was before, even though his earnings may be very low. He may also enjoy greater esteem within the family because he is bringing in a little money and thus contributing to its upkeep. He looks upon himself as more grown up than other children of his age because, as well as working and mixing with adults and being paid a little money for what he does, he can to some extent decide himself how he is going to spend the part of his wages that his parents give back to him to cover his expenses. All this gives him a feeling of importance and greater independence, as some Italian writers have shown. [2] To increase this feeling of independence he often falls into the trap of trying to compensate for his small physical size, his poverty and his lack of basic needs by incurring extravagant expenses and indulging in bad habits (smoking, gambling, etc.).

However, the seemingly positive aspects of child labour are quickly and fully countered by the immediate problems they bring in their train. First, the working child has no time for playing, or at least for playing enough, nor for taking healthy exercise—and this at a time of life when these activities are so important for his future development. Second, hours of work and school hours generally clash, and in many cases the need to work puts any idea of attendance at school out of the question; in other cases, the child's tiredness and lack of concentration are reflected in his repeated failure and lack of progress at school. Third, because he does not have the time or the energy to learn, the working child cannot develop his mental faculties. Fourth, as a result of his lack of development and early entry into unskilled working life, his aspirations quickly become fixed at a very low level.

The child worker's extreme fatigue is due to the fact that his powers of resistance and his muscular strength are below those of adults ; when he is obliged to exert himself as much as they do, at the same speed and without any extra work breaks, it is only to be expected that he should feel more tired than they. [3]

In industrial and commercial milieux the child's normal sensitivity, coupled with his poor conditions of work, increase the difficulties he has in adapting himself to a new and complex pattern of human relationships. But these difficulties may not only be subjective : he may also not be made welcome, unkind jokes may be played on him, he may be ill treated and may be left out of the adult workers' conversation during breaks.

Work in the streets is generally less difficult for a child. However, problems do arise (apart from occupational problems), for example when the child has to compete with more experienced adults, when he is threatened by groups of youths or adults who demand a percentage of his takings or when he falls into bad company and drifts into vagrancy, begging, drug addiction and drug-running, delinquency, sexual deviance, prostitution, and so on. Interestingly enough, as long ago as 1912 Edward Clopper listed the effects that street work could have on children, under three headings : material, physical and moral deterioration. [4] Under "material deterioration" three effects are suggested: that the child may acquire a distaste for regular employment ; that he has small chance of acquiring a trade ; and that he may drift into a large class of casual workers. The effects due to "physical deterioration" are given as : night work ; excessive fatigue ; exposure to bad weather ; irregularity of sleep and meals ; use of stimulants (cigarettes, coffee, alcohol) ; and disease through contact with vice. The following effects are listed under "moral deterioration" : the child may be encouraged to play truant ; he may show independence and defiance of parental control ; he may develop weaknesses cultivated by the formation of bad habits ; he may form a liking for "petty excitements of the street" ; opportunities may arise for him to drift into delinquency ; and street work furnishes a large percentage of the recruits to the criminal population.

In addition to occupational risks as such, the various jobs that a child does expose his frail body to a wide range of complaints, ranging from headaches, coughs and colds, hearing disorders and visual fatigue to fever and advanced lung diseases.

The younger the child is, the more serious most of these problems become, because he is less strong (and hence more vulnerable) and because he is more easily influenced. Further, the lack of concern shown by some parents, coupled with the lack of healthy exercise and physical recreation, non-attendance at school, the fatigue caused by work, the unhappy experiences of, in particular, children who work on the streets (which can mark them for the rest of their lives), the illnesses that their weakened bodies may contract, and the occupational accidents to which they are exposed because of their lack of self-discipline, makes the risk of their material, physical and moral deterioration greater still.

Since it is the normal thing for these underprivileged children to work, or at least to look for work, it would be a contradiction to say that the fact that they do work sets them apart from other people in some way. However, there is no doubt but that child workers, irrespective of their actual numbers and the percentage of the total population that they represent, are on the fringe of society, when society is construed of being composed of groups of persons more skilled than they are and having greater social influence. This results from their narrow outlook, which itself is a result of their lack of education and vocational training and their own increasing awareness of the gap that separates them from other social and occupational groups.

REPERCUSSIONS OF CHILD LABOUR

Social and labour repercussions

How will the child worker of today fare, from the social and labour viewpoint, in the years to come ? This will depend very much on the character of the child in question, the kind of job he is doing, the circumstances in which he is doing it, and his personal hopes for the future. Although often these hopes are inevitably far from high, working children do sometimes manage to set up as employers themselves or succeed in graduating to more skilled work. As a general rule, however, when a child performs stultifying, precarious and insignificant work from an early age, this prevents (or at least considerably hinders) his acquiring any genuine qualifications for more skilled work. This, together with the lack of inclination to learn that stems from his immaturity, effectively puts an end to his chances of better employment, higher pay and social advancement. It is therefore very likely that a man who has been at work from an early age will spend his whole life at the bottom of the social ladder, performing routine, unskilled jobs, when he is not out of work altogether.

Physical repercussions

Many of the jobs that children do are harmful for their physical development. Their growing bodies suffer continually from the effects of fatigue, over-exertion, lack of hygiene and all the other problems with which they are confronted. For example, excessive heat, work in bad weather and continuous contact with dust cause morbid conditions that are more or less chronic and are difficult to cure : skin troubles, bronchitis, tuberculosis, and so on.

Many jobs done by children are the cause of physical deformities and various illnesses, or else they aggravate defects or maladies such as heart disease, affections of the throat, flat fcet, and so on.

An interesting experiment was carried out recently in Japan on young workers and students. [5] It was found that until they reached the age of 12 there was no difference in height between children in the two groups ; however, those who began to work before they were 14 years old were subsequently found, on average, to be 4 cm shorter than the students who had not entered working life until after they were 18 years old.

Heavy loads and awkward body positions in particular can affect physical growth—especially the growth of the bones, which are still soft in children. When a child is regularly bent double under a heavy burden or is obliged to stay in an unnatural position for long periods, deformation of the spinal column, pelvis and/or thorax may be the result. This is because before puberty the strength, powers of resistance and physical defences of children of both sexes are proportionally lower the younger they are. During the years leading up to and during puberty the immature organism is constantly growing ; it undergoes regular endocrinal and vegetative changes which are adversely affected by certain types of fatigue—especially continuous and excessive fatigue—and by unhealthy and dangerous conditions. [6]

In the less developed regions the malnutrition of the majority of working children, the fatigue, lack of proteins and amino-acids, and the anaemia and other affections from which they often suffer, can seriously damage the central nervous system.

It is thus clear, and has been scientifically proved, that, in the conditions in which it is usually carried out, the employment of children (not to mention the frequent risks of occupational accidents and diseases as such) is both directly and indirectly harmful for the child, and its results will be carried over into adult life.

Mental repercussions

When a young child begins to work, and especially when he leaves the family circle to do so, the parents must be doubly vigilant, since the age at which he usually starts to work coincides more or less with a period of profound mental change in the child. Clearly, if to the working child's unfavourable intellectual status is added an ill directed mental development, there will be undesirable consequences and behaviour problems, caused by the child's inadequate comprehension of the adult world and by his imitating, distorting and exaggerating what he wrongly believes to be the essence of that world. These failings, linked with his lack of adequate general education and vocational training, restrict his ability to make a significant contribution to the social milieu in which he lives.

The normal needs and tendencies of puberty and adolescence, which instead of being satisfied are converted into a premature "pseudo"-maturity, have a permanent limiting and disturbing effect on the psychological life of the adult. Again, the feeling of injustice and frustration, stemming from their inability to do what others do and be on the same intellectual level as others, can have a permanent effect on personal relationships and even lead to aberrations of behaviour and personality.

THE EXPLOITATION OF CHILDREN:
AN UNNATURAL SITUATION [7]

In a child who starts to work full time, or for whom work becomes the most important element in his life, and under conditions of exploitation, a set of reflexes and physical changes is triggered off which marks an abrupt and unnatural transformation from childhood to premature adulthood. By forcing him to work, the social milieu which envelops him virtually compels him to leave his childhood behind—that is, to abandon the motivations, problems and interests that are characteristic of childhood.

One of the most obvious activities of childhood is "play"—a spontaneous, free, uncontrolled, non-productive outburst of energy. The child worker cannot give free rein to this entirely natural urge, which consequently withers away for lack of use. Sometimes these childish pastimes are replaced by others that more resemble adult games, in which the "play" element nevertheless emerges but in an attenuated form in order not to appear too childish. Thus the games in which children play at being "grown-ups" suddenly stop, because the child worker is in fact playing an adult role in earnest.

Young children usually have vivid imaginations and may live in a fantasy world. There is no place for these in the world of work, so they fade away in the working child's mind, to be promptly replaced by the practical realities that mark the world of production and services. The child's creativeness and ability to transcend reality are thus blunted, and his whole mental world is thus impoverished.

The indecision and changeability that are so characteristic of childhood give way to a rapid and precocious crystallisation of the sudden need to adopt adult attitudes.

The irresponsible elements in a child's nature must also be curtailed or eliminated altogether when he begins to work, since he is obliged to carry out specific tasks in a set way, so as not to cause accidents, spoil material or reduce quality or productivity, and so that he may earn enough to live on and not be dismissed. The responsibilities that bear on him also lead to premature economic worries that are unhealthy for the present and future wellbeing of himself and his family.

When all the elements that are characteristic of childhood are combined, the result is recreational play—something typical of childhood that the working child cannot enjoy. Indeed, if he does not behave in a way that is contrary to his natural inclinations, if he does not bring all his concentration to bear on the job that has been assigned to him, inter alia the risk of accidents is increased.

It is only to be expected that such constant pressure on him to abandon his childhood has a powerful effect on his nervous system. And if, by chance, the childish elements in the child worker's personality manage to elude the repression or distortion to which they are subjected and to blossom out into the behaviour, attitudes or expressions of childhood, or if these elements obstruct the smooth running of the production operations, his employer and his adult fellow-workers disapprove of his conduct, and this can have a strong effect at the emotional level. The child immediately takes the criticism to heart, without understanding its true social function—that is, to ensure the smooth running of material operations carried on for profit.

Notes

[1] For further information on the implications of rapid population growth for the training, employment and welfare of workers and on the ILO's activities in population matters, see ILO : *Population and labour* (Geneva, 1973).

[2] Piccione, op. cit., pp. 47-48 ; Rosa Miragliotta : "I minori del 'Borgo vecchio' a Palermo", in *Esperienze Sociali* (Palermo), July 1977 ; *Libro bianco sul lavoro minorile* (Rome, Edizioni ACLI, 1967).

[3] H. Desoille : *La médecine du travail,* Collection "Que sais-je ?" (Paris, Presses Universitaires de France, 1967), p. 76.

[4] Clopper, op. cit., pp. 128-129.

[5] Desoille, op. cit., pp. 76-77.

[6] *La medicina sociale per i fanciulli ed i giovani,* Proceedings of a seminar held in Bari, 24-25 May 1971 (Rome, Istituto Italiano di Medicina Sociale, 1971), p. 9.

[7] This section draws heavily on Mauro Quinzi : "Aspetti psicopedagogici del lavoro minorile", Part 2, in *Problemi Minorili* (Rome), Nov.-Dec. 1969.

EDUCATION AND TRAINING

6

GENERAL EDUCATION

In the less developed regions the provision of education to children, as an alternative to their going out to work, gives rise to a number of serious problems. To begin with, there is a severe shortage of schools, particularly in rural areas, where those that do exist are few and far between. Again, only a very small number of schools provide full-time courses ; the great majority are used by two or more sets of pupils, precisely because of this shortage of school accommodation. Consequently, even if all children of school age were allowed or able to attend school for the full period of compulsory schooling, they could not do so because there would be no school for them to go to. In Indonesia, for example, as shown in Chapter 11, the shortage of schools seems to be the main reason why children go out to work. Again, in most of Africa the achievement of compulsory education for all is still many years away. Children of school age who actually go to school are in the minority, and as these pupils grow older more and more of them leave the school. This trend is even more apparent as one moves from urban to rural areas, since children in the country leave school at an earlier age than those in the town. In India it has been calculated that by the end of the current Five-Year Plan no more than 50 per cent of children between the ages of 11 and 14 will be receiving full-time compulsory schooling. [1] The percentage is even lower elsewhere in Asia and in several countries of Latin America.

Thus, despite the tremendous efforts being made by the Third World countries to make school education available to all, the idea of compulsory education is still a pure academic exercise. There are still vast numbers of people who are either illiterate or semi-literate—and this includes not only children of school age but adults as well.

In those places where there is a school many children cannot attend because they have to work ; others combine school with work, usually to the detriment of their performance at school ; many cannot attend school for the simple reason that their parents do not have enough money to buy them the books and other materials they need (see, for instance, Chapter 10) ; and indeed the parents of some children are opposed to the very idea of their going to school. Thus, we may summarise the various categories as follows :

children who go to school and do not work ; those who both go to school and work ; those who do not go to school but work (or consider themselves unemployed) ; those who neither work nor go to school ; and those who go to school for a few years and then leave to be able to devote themselves entirely to work.

Many parents prefer to send their sons to school rather than their daughters, in the belief that there is no point in a girl studying since her job in life will be to get married, to do unskilled work or simply to stay at home.

In rural areas not only do fewer children go to school because of a general shortage of school premises and because of stronger traditional objections on the part of their parents, but a good proportion of those who do attend eventually stop doing so, for various reasons, which may act singly or in combination. For instance, school terms may clash with the major agricultural cycles (especially sowing and harvesting) and temporary absence from school may result—following which it may be difficult to pick up the educational threads, or the child may simply leave school once and for all. In any case, those rural families whose children go to school want them to complete their compulsory schooling as soon as possible, so that they may help the rest of the family with its agricultural work. Thus the parents' attitude not only restricts the attendance of their children at school but simultaneously encourages them to drop out.

In general, then, we may say that the reasons for giving up school are more or less the same as those for not sending the children to school in the first place (see Chapters 12 and 13).

Drop-outs are more frequent in the least developed regions, amongst girls, in rural areas and in slums.

Rural parents have a tendency to look upon the education provided by the school as being purely academic and thus inappropriate for their needs, if not an unnecessary luxury in which they cannot allow themselves to indulge. As well as not understanding the evident advantages that their children gain from education, rural families often resist sending them to school because of the high percentage of failures. These failures are largely caused by the fact that the pupil's interests are different from those inculcated by the school and also by the fatigue resulting from agricultural work.

Nevertheless, in many regions of the Third World, and despite traditional attitudes and all the other problems, many parents believe that it *is* necessary for their children to have some form of schooling ; some parents manage to realise their hopes, but others, bowed down by poverty, are obliged to take their children away from school and set them to work.

The problem of absence from school is almost insoluble with regard to nomadic peoples ; their seasonal migrations cause difficulties greater than any of those mentioned hitherto.

The children of migrant agricultural workers, whether or not they work themselves, encounter greater difficulties in attending school than other children, not only because of all the problems that underprivileged children in general have to face but also because of the need to change schools and/or the difficulty of finding a school in the vicinity.

Very many parents who are not especially interested in the education of their children nevertheless send them to school for a couple of years or so— in principle between the ages of 6 and 9—not with the intention that they should acquire at least the rudiments of education but simply to keep them away from the home, in the belief that they are more trouble than they are worth. When they reach the age of 9 they are stronger, more mature and more disciplined, and the parents take them away from school so that they can work either within or outside the family circle.

Compulsory schooling is, of course, incompatible with the practice of sending children out to work. The years during which the child should be at school ought to be years of productive and genuine attendance and not years of intellectual impoverishment in an unskilled job. Studying and learning can open many doors, raise the child's hopes for the future, improve his output, eliminate mental and cultural backwardness and outmoded traditions, and so on. The school, together with the education a child receives at home, should be a preparation for life in his specific socio-cultural context. When the child cannot, for one reason or another, receive this introduction to life at home, when his non-attendance at school leaves a yawning gap in his development and when he is thrown on to the labour market at an early age, his introduction to life will be influenced by the groups he may chance to mix with and by undisciplined elements he may meet on the streets or at his workplace, with easily imaginable results.

In the more advanced countries, on the other hand, practically all children go to school. Indeed, the degree of development of a country seems to be linked with the proportion of its children who attend school.

VOCATIONAL TRAINING

In the less developed regions the school curriculum, as an extension of that process begun in the home whereby the child learns the habits and beliefs of the society in which he lives, ought to include some practical education appropriate to the socio-cultural environment in which he lives. Such education could be linked with a little light work. In fact, one cannot speak of true vocational training for children of school age, because the minimum age at which an apprenticeship may legally be begun generally corresponds to the (theoretical) age at which compulsory schooling ends. However, in a good number of countries it is customary for children of about 10 years of age to become apprentices in a handicrafts workshop, where they will learn a trade at the workplace itself : carpet manufacturing, pottery, various traditional crafts. In fact, practically the same system operates on those premises where the most varied types of modern industrial activity are carried out : car repairs and other mechanical engineering services, building trades, jobs in the clothing industry, and so on.

In these workshops the children learn their trade as they work, or else they are employed as apprentices, with no payment being made for their output. (We have already mentioned the numerous abuses to which this employment relationship can give rise.) It has been claimed that in certain circumstances and contexts this kind of on-the-job training is more effective than that given in technical institutes (see Chapter 12).

The length of time that this traditional method of apprenticeship lasts varies considerably, depending on such factors as the difficulty of the job to be learnt and whether or not the employer-instructor is available to teach it. In reality, and taking these factors into account, one must distinguish between the time the child really needs to learn the trade thoroughly and the time during which the employer wants him to maintain his status as an apprentice, irrespective of the degree of skill he may have acquired. Generally speaking, a traditional type of apprenticeship, served by a young person at the workplace before he reaches the age at which he may legally begin an "official" apprenticeship, or before he reaches the minimum age for admission to employment, may last for two, three or four years (see Chapter 15).

This traditional, informal training is usually even more informal when the fathers, other members of the family or family friends provide it, since it is then reduced to a minimum of observation and imitation.

It should be pointed out here that many of the jobs that children do (street traders, shoeblacks, delivery boys, assistants in small businesses, car park attendants, newspaper sellers, petrol station attendants, etc., in fixed locations) are learnt very quickly because they call for no special skills. In such cases "on-the-job training" is reduced to its simplest elements and gives the child no specific training for the future (see Chapters 12 and 13). If the situation of the young apprentice who is learning a genuine trade is hard, that of the children in the categories we have mentioned is even worse, because they will be faced with the future life of unemployment, of under-employment or, in the best cases, of unskilled jobs.

There is a great difference—as regards both vocational training and work itself—between the situation of those children who are obliged to work and those who are purposely excluded from the scope of Convention No. 138, because they do their work in schools for general, vocational or technical education or in other training institutions, where such work is carried out in accordance with prescribed conditions and is an integral part of *(a)* a course of education or training for which a school or training institution is primarily responsible ; *(b)* a programme of training mainly or entirely in an undertaking and which has been approved by the competent authority ; or *(c)* a programme of guidance or orientation designed to facilitate the choice of an occupation or of a line of training.

Note

[1] Singh, Kaura and Khan, op. cit., p. 15.

FUTURE ACTION

7

In the preceding pages we have looked at the different facets of child labour : the present situation and extent of the problem, the dangers it brings in its train, the harm it causes, its evil repercussions on the whole future life of the child worker, the relevant legislation (and its gaps and shortcomings), the lack of schooling that it entails and in general the poverty which is its root cause in the majority of cases. The most pressing needs now are that the world as a whole should understand the nature of this scourge and that concrete measures should be taken to deal with it, in both the long and the short terms.

Short-term measures should aim basically at improving the conditions of work and life of those young people who form part of the labour force. Of course, these measures should be sufficiently flexible to meet any subsequent structural changes that may affect child labour. And it is in fact these structural changes (which, as we shall see, are wide ranging) that will determine the form taken by the long-term measures, the true purpose of which will not be to improve the conditions of working children but rather to bring about gradually a world-wide dénouement to the tragedy of child labour—a dénouement that will be nothing less than its total and final abolition.

If the situation is to evolve along these lines, the following steps seem to be important :

(a) it must be made quite clear that the child is not built to undertake stultifying work, because he is not sufficiently developed physically and mentally to be able to cope adequately with the demands made on him by work ; on the contrary, he needs to lead a life in which education and recreation play a large part. In short, the child is not a "small adult", nor he is a machine or beast of burden ;

(b) attempts must be made to enforce the existing legislation aiming at the progressive elimination of child labour and to complement this legislation with practical measures of social policy ;

(c) as long as this legislation, in the form it takes at present, is unsuccessful in eliminating child labour, the existing conditions of work and life of the working child must be improved by all possible means, thus breaking down the state of helplessness into which, paradoxically, the present legislation flings him ;

(d) measures of an economic nature must be taken to eliminate gradually the necessity for children to work ;

(e) steps must be taken to extend compulsory schooling to all ;

(f) the trade unions must be encouraged to fight child labour and to campaign for its elimination and thus indirectly for increased employment opportunities and higher wages for adult workers ;

(g) nation-wide information campaigns must be organised in all countries to bring home to the population the ill-effects of child labour and the alternatives to it ; and

(h) a wind of change must blow through society and through the minds of men, for it is only if men adopt a radical new outlook that the ultimate aim, the elimination of child labour, can be achieved.

Let us now examine these proposals in greater detail.

THE CHILD IS NOT A "SMALL ADULT"

Contrary to what many people believe, the child's body and mind are not sufficiently developed for him to work without their suffering damage. Unfortunately, the general public is largely unaware of this fact. The general public must therefore be taught that whilst, on the one hand, the child willingly carries out little jobs for his parents—jobs which form part of the socialisation process and which, moreover, makes him feel that he is useful and that he is sharing in the family effort—on the other hand, "work" as such has an irreversible effect on his health and constitution and mortgages his whole future. The general public must also be made aware of the fact that, to ensure his balanced development, it is essential not only that the child must *not* work but also that he must have the opportunity to play. Work is often harmful for a child ; healthy recreation is of benefit to him and enriches his life.

Study and learning, which broaden his horizons, are other beneficial elements in a child's life. Those parents who force their children to work—especially those who do not bother to send them to school—must be made fully aware of the fact that they are ruining the life of their offspring for the sake of a few coppers. The child is not a "small adult", nor a machine, nor a beast of burden : he is a new shoot on the family tree, a shoot that needs to grow firm and strong, and it is unthinkable that society, and above all his own parents, should not even know what the right conditions are for this shoot to develop. Today's child is, in fact, the future of the world.

LEGAL AND PRACTICAL MEANS OF PROGRESSIVELY ELIMINATING CHILD LABOUR

We have already seen that, in the developing countries especially, the enforcement of the existing laws prohibiting the employment of children is hampered by serious problems due to poverty, traditional attitudes and the difficulty of replacing child labour by adult labour.

If the law were fully observed the result would be the complete protection of the child against exploitation and, at the same time, the protection of the employment and income of adults. This situation is clearly foreseen, in all its many aspects, in the provisions of Convention No. 138 and the accompanying Recommendation No. 146. Member States of the ILO who ratify this Convention undertake "to pursue a national policy designed to ensure the effective abolition of child labour and to raise progressively the minimum age for admission to employment or work to a level consistent with the fullest physical and mental development of young persons". If they are to achieve these aims, each of the countries concerned will need to introduce far-reaching and clear-cut social policy programmes, in which the various stages of their implementation are clearly laid down.

As the poverty of those children who are obliged to work is often associated with a somewhat disorganised family life, with non-attendance at school and with a lack of healthy recreation, these social policy programmes might tackle such questions head on (the problem of non-attendance at school will be dealt with below).

Turning first to possible methods of reducing the poverty of the family and, ultimately, of taking the children out of the labour market altogether, one could envisage paying family allowances to needy families, which would be granted on condition that the children should carry out no form of paid, family or self-employed work at all and that they should attend school instead.

As economic distress and frustration lead to strained family relationships, disorganised family life, alcoholism, vagrancy and other related problems, other means of strengthening the unity of the family, besides the allowances mentioned above, must be investigated. These include other forms of social assistance, which could perhaps be provided by professional, state or charitable organisations or by the religious bodies with which the people identify. In many countries this would be a socially very useful way of occupying the educated unemployed.

Children from irremediably broken homes, who are sent out from an early age to roam the streets and to carry out desultory jobs and who often drift into delinquency, should be able to turn for help to specialised institutions which in effect replace the home, provide them with an atmosphere of affection and welcome and look after their education and training. Institutions of this kind do exist in many countries but, as their running often leaves much to be desired, they do not really carry out the functions for which they were created.

In all countries of the less developed regions facilities for healthy recreation are extremely scarce, where they are not absent altogether. For the sake of the balanced development of the child a tremendous effort is called for in this respect.

If we are not to lose ourselves in Utopian digressions, we must consider the source of the funds that would make these various social programmes possible. Some countries do have the necessary means at their disposal ; most developing countries, however, do not. Everything will turn on the importance which the developing countries ascribe to having a generation of young people who are healthy and educated, on a determined political will and on a radical change in priorities in their respective national budgets. In this the developing countries must not stand alone. In the words of the resolution concerning the International Year of the Child and the progressive elimination of child labour and transitional measures, adopted by the International Labour Conference in June 1979, [1] it will be necessary "to develop international solidarity and co-operation with the developing countries and to activate efforts to establish a new and fair international economic order so as to respond more effectively to the basic measures undertaken by each State for better child protection".

LEGAL AND PRACTICAL MEANS OF IMPROVING THE WORKING CONDITIONS OF CHILD WORKERS

Even though all possible measures may be taken to apply the principles of international labour standards and of the corresponding national legislation, it cannot be overlooked that for the time being a very large number of children do work throughout the world in the appalling conditions described in earlier chapters and that, therefore, protective measures must be devised to look after these children.

It is self-evident that when child labour is purely and simply prohibited by law, the law cannot then introduce measures to protect child workers, since legally they do not exist. In view of the impotence of the present legislation and until this can assume the truly protective role for which it was devised, there is a need for measures which, instead of paying no heed to reality (especially the reality in the less developed regions), should face up to that reality. Not only is this a benefit in itself, as it is in the case of adult workers, but also it cannot but contribute to reducing the evil effects of premature work on the health, growth and future life of working children.

As a first step, each country should adopt measures designed to afford genuine protection to child workers. These measures must be adapted to the circumstances, traditions and types of work found in each country and be applied in the light of these. They could provide for tax reductions, subsidies and other kinds of bonus for those employers who show that they are improving the working conditions of the children they employ. As it is quite impossible to engage enough labour inspectors to go round all the many undertakings in the informal and agricultural sectors where most children work, the help of the various social assistance organisations mentioned above could be enlisted to draw the attention of the labour inspection services to the most flagrant cases of the exploitation of child workers.

Of course, the adoption of measures of this kind means facing up to reality and recognising implicitly that illegal child labour does exist. Once this is generally recognised, there should be no shortage either of suggestions for its gradual elimination or of measures to improve the working conditions of children while it lasts.

There is a difference between the problem of illegal child labour and that of children whose work is legal—that is, of those children who work after they have reached the minimum age for admission to employment in countries where that age is lower than that laid down in international labour standards. In such cases, on the one hand the minimum age must be raised ; and, on the other, until this happens the working conditions of these children should be improved. This can be done by introducing shorter working hours and equal pay for equal work, arranging for their attendance at general and vocational training courses, prohibiting their lifting excessively heavy loads, and introducing a wide variety of special protective measures, on the grounds that, although in their own countries young people are legally able to undertake adult work, physically and mentally they are not capable of doing so.

ECONOMIC MEASURES

People have become more and more aware in recent years that an increase in GNP does not lead automatically to the underprivileged classes, particularly in developing countries, deriving any benefit from that increase. Economic policies pursued by regional, national and international bodies must not aim solely at an increase in GNP but must also be based on the recognition of the "fundamental criteria for development : full employment, accelerated and balanced growth, satisfaction of basic needs, and more socially just patterns of income distribution" ; [2] for the fight against child labour is but one aspect of the over-all fight against poverty. Thus, when their misery is eradicated, when their fathers have a job that is rewarded more fairly and when their standard of living is raised, school-age children will no longer be obliged to go out to work.

COMPULSORY SCHOOLING FOR ALL

Attendance at school should not be a virtually unattainable ideal for those children who come from the poorer social classes or who live in rural areas. Nor should the number of children without adequate education be increased by school drop-outs. Universal compulsory education should be one of the permanent features of national life. Instead of sinking into intellectual inertia and spending all their lives in dead-end jobs, children should develop their minds at school—to use the UNESCO aphorism, they should "learn to be". One remembers here the spectacular progress made since the introduction of universal compulsory education in those countries which are now the most economically advanced in the world.

In many Third World countries one often hears the complaint that education is traditional, theoretical and academic, that it is slanted towards specific social classes, and that it is looked upon as useless by many who live in country areas—that is, it is not adapted to the daily working needs of the local population, especially the rural population. It is certainly true that the content of education should be adapted in part to meet local needs and should contain practical elements, including a certain amount of "pre-vocational" training. During this "pre-vocational" stage the children could begin to do productive work—not, however, under conditions of deadening exploitation but in the best possible circumstances. This would at the same time enable them to find a job, undertake skilled work, earn higher wages and, in the end, make their way towards a better life. Furthermore, in rural areas the timing of the school year must take account of agricultural and stock-breeding production cycles, so that pupils can help their parents by doing light jobs for short periods, without having to miss school.

Despite the many voices raised to the contrary, however, it seems unnecessary to change direction completely and to provide an exclusively pragmatic form of education, for general culture is both necessary and beneficial : everyone should have access to it, and it is essential to imbue pupils with a liking for it. The ideal formula for the countries in question would seem to be a combination of a general cultural education with elements of practical knowledge.

THE ROLE OF THE TRADE UNIONS

As working children are not often members of trade unions, they have no power to bargain over their conditions of work ; and as in any case the law does not recognise the existence of their work, there is no organised and forceful body to concern itself with removing them from the labour force altogether. Up to the present time, with a few notable exceptions, national trade unions in the developing countries have not always paid sufficient attention to child workers. It is nevertheless very important that they should insist on the application of the existing legislation on the minimum age for admission to employment, with a view to the gradual elimination of child labour. Three reasons should suffice to convince them of the need for this : (a) the physical and mental havoc that is wrought by child labour ; (b) the fact that each child worker is effectively employed in place of an adult worker ; and (c) the fact that child labour reduces adult earnings.

Many individual adult workers would resist the adoption of measures of this kind and would prefer to continue turning a blind eye to the problem, since they themselves, dogged by poverty, believe that it is a sound policy to send their children out to earn a little money. In spite of this, if trade unions fully comprehend the problem and are determined to tackle it vigorously, positive results should be forthcoming before too much time has elapsed.

INFORMATION CAMPAIGNS

All those involved in child labour—that is, the child workers themselves, their parents, their employers, social assistance institutions, trade unions and governments—should be made fully aware both of the harm and damage that work can do to child workers, to the society of which they are a part and to the generations to come, and of the benefits that may be derived from the alternative solutions put forward here. They should also realise the difference between light, educational work, on the one hand, and harmful exploitation, on the other. In many cases this knowledge can dissuade the most directly involved parties from having recourse to the exploitation of young people.

To make this information widely known, governments should launch regular information and education campaigns, using posters, leaflets, slogans, and so on. Radio, television and the press, either on their own initiative or in association with the government or at its suggestion, could run similar campaigns.

Research institutions could study in detail the various tasks that children undertake in a country, and publish a full analysis of the possible or certain, temporary or chronic repercussions on the life and physical and mental health of children that result from the practice of each of these tasks. These studies should not be written for scholars alone but should be disseminated as widely as possible among the general public.

Public lectures could be organised for the same purpose, illustrated by colour slides wherever possible.

It would perhaps be advisable for a government body—possibly the labour inspectorate—to co-ordinate these activities on behalf of all those taking part in them.

EVOLUTION OF SOCIETY

The exploitation of children is found for the most part in those human societies which have to satisfy their immediate basic needs within a modern marginal framework or within a modernisation programme. The economy, the social organisation and the traditional mentality are the three elements making up these societies and they interact to perpetuate a situation of which child labour is one component. This social phenomenon is in fact a reflection of other important phenomena, and the solution to the problem lies rather with the orderly development of society than with the adoption of a particular norm or standard. [3] Thus the solution is ultimately to be found in a modification of the three elements mentioned above. This modification will be induced by making people aware of the problem rather than by imposing an external solution. The gradual elimination of child labour is a large-scale task that will not be achieved in isolation from other social changes but will be an integral part of them. Many times during the history of mankind, whole peoples have been induced to change their economy, their social organisation and/or their traditional mentality. The overcoming of resistance to change (carried out, however, by rational and peaceful methods) will accelerate the achievement of the desired results.

In concrete terms, whatever the national situation may be, it falls to individual governments to set as their target the structural changes that seem essential, bearing in mind the present state of society, its needs and its aspirations. It should be mentioned here that the measures proposed in this chapter reflect those in the ILO's major programme on meeting basic needs, and, in particular, reflect its concern for the principle of equal pay for equal work, for the principle that vocational training and working conditions appropriate to the age of those involved should be made available, and for the gradual elimination of child labour ; and reflect the emphasis laid by this programme on the importance of education, which is itself considered to be one of the basic needs of mankind.

Notes

[1] See Appendix E.

[2] Resolution concerning follow-up to the World Employment Conference adopted by the International Labour Conference at its 65th Session, Geneva, 1979.

[3] See Luciana Marsili Sarto : "Gli infortuni nel lavoro abusivo dei fanciulli", in *Ragazzi d'Oggi* (Rome), Dec. 1971.

PART II

SOME ASPECTS OF CHILD LABOUR
IN TEN COUNTRIES

ARGENTINA

Centre for Labour Studies and Research (CEIL),
Buenos Aires *

8

SOCIOCULTURAL BACKGROUND

The high concentration of people in the towns and cities of Argentina contrasts with the very low proportion of the economically active population working in agriculture (14.8 per cent). The average annual income per head is US$1,920, [1] the life expectancy is 66 years [2] and the proportion of illiterates is low (7 per cent). The crude birth rate too is low (22 per thousand between 1965 and 1970), [3] as is the proportion of young people—the national population census of 1970 indicates that the 0 to 14 age-group accounted for 29.1 per cent of the total population at that time.

The pampas region is the most developed area, both as regards agriculture and in the concentration of industry, commerce and services. Approximately 70 per cent of the population live in the city of Buenos Aires and the five adjacent provinces (Buenos Aires, Córdoba, Entre Ríos, Santa Fe and La Pampa). It was here that the majority of the immigrants from southern Europe settled at the end of the nineteenth century and early in the twentieth, causing a fundamental change in the social and demographic structure of the country. Subsequently, large numbers of internal migrants settled in and around metropolitan Buenos Aires, thus accentuating the sharply defined division of the country into densely populated urban and sparsely populated rural areas.

The remaining regions of the country vary considerably in physical structure, climate, economic function and type of social structure. We may summarise the main categories as follows :

(a) "islands of development", which reproduce in certain small areas the privileged conditions of the pampas region ;

(b) enclaves where intensive agro-industrial or agricultural activities create jobs (even though these are frequently of a casual nature) and are a factor

---

* Centre for Labour Studies and Research, National Council for Scientific and Technical Research, Buenos Aires.

for economic growth, although conditions of work and income distribution are commonly below standard ;

(c) areas which, for reasons of geography and climate (basically because of their aridity), offer few opportunities for production and which are reservoirs of labour for casual agricultural work in more favoured areas ;

(d) rural areas with large numbers of small farms, to which workers from neighbouring countries come to undertake temporary and casual agricultural jobs ; these areas are many and varied, but are particularly common in type *(b)* and *(c)* regions ;

(e) urban concentrations in the regions described briefly above ; these differ as regards the functions they carry out in their area of influence and as regards their production base. Job opportunities are limited in all of them, however, owing to internal migration and immigration from neighbouring countries.

The situation of children in Argentina should be set against these different backgrounds. Three population types may be distinguished in the most developed urban regions :

(a) upper- and middle-class sectors, characterised by families with a small number of children. Education is highly prized here (completed secondary and even university education is the general ideal), and entry into the labour market takes place only when the youngster has passed through the adolescent stage ;

(b) popular sectors, of which the boundary with the middle-class sector, in this country with considerable social mobility, is relatively ill defined (consider, for example, the position of skilled and self-employed or family workers). Here the composition of the family does not differ greatly from that of middle-class families, and here too the value of education is recognised. There are differences, however. Thus, whilst we may point to the trend towards a higher level of education (including vocational and technical training), it is also true that at the lower end of this sector a considerable number of children make an early entry into the labour market (round about the end of primary education, at 13 or 14 years of age), for instance if they do not make sufficiently good progress at school and/or if the economic situation of the family demands it ;

(c) "marginal" or poor sectors, which again are separated from the sector above by a relatively ill defined dividing line, but which are characterised by a more unstable occupational and/or residential status. In these groups, which are often composed of more recent migrants from underdeveloped rural areas, both in Argentina itself and in neighbouring countries, there tend to be more children per family. The parents' concern for education, its possibilities and its value for the specific needs of this group is limited, and for this reason it is to be expected that the children will make an

early entry into the labour market ; thus the main body of child workers in urban areas is to be found in this population sector. Two specific points need to be brought out here : first, the rural tradition of employment at an early age, by which the whole family contributes to the family income, is carried over to urban areas ; and second, the darker side of the picture, this comparatively healthy situation degenerates into the exploitation of children in begging and in street trading or other activities which are tantamount to begging. In the urban areas of the non-pampas provinces this population sector is of considerable size, and "marginal" child labour has taken on the dimensions of a social problem.

In rural areas also it is necessary to distinguish zones and strata. [4] Thus, family producers of the pampas region and some irrigated zones, the descendants of the southern European migrants mentioned above, exploit their holdings through an intensive use of family labour. During the past few decades, however, the intensive mechanisation of agricultural work [5] has had a greater influence on this occupational group than on any other. As a result, child labour here is much less common, and the educational level has risen considerably. The situation is different in the other agricultural regions where, moreover, the fertility rates are much higher, mechanisation is less intensive and family employment (including child labour) is widespread— with, as we shall see, an adverse effect on the formal education of the children.

Special reference must be made here to those workers mentioned above who are engaged in the cycle of temporary and casual agricultural jobs and who eke out their existence in very poor living and working conditions. The children of these workers, together with those involved in marginal activities in urban areas, are among the least favoured in the whole country. On the one hand, the nomadic life affects their possibility of schooling. On the other, it is common for the family labour force to be employed on tasks that call for considerable physical effort, as part of the employment obligations of each family.

SOME DATA ON POPULATION

After the great wave of European immigrants who arrived in Argentina at the end of the last century had been absorbed, the average age of the population began to rise. A marked downward trend in the crude birth rate led to a reduction in the proportion of those in the under-14 age-group. This trend was already visible in the 1914 census (40.1 per cent), but "it was between 1914 and 1947 that the greatest reduction in the relative importance of the youngest age-groups occurred (0-14 years = 30.9 per cent). Since 1947 the process has slowed down somewhat and the most significant change has been in the over-64 age-group, whose numbers more than doubled between 1947

Table 4.   Argentina : percentage distribution and growth rates for various age-groups, 1960 and 1970

Age-group	Year		Growth rate 1960-70
	1960	1970	
Up to 9	21.0	20.0	1.61
10-14	9.7	9.4	1.27
15-19	8.4	9.0	2.18
20-64	55.0	54.7	1.51
65 and above	5.6	6.9	3.64
Total	100.0	100.0	1.55

Source. 1960 and 1970 national population censuses.

and 1960." [6] If we compare the censuses of 1960 and 1970 we can see the extent to which the proportion of children and young persons in the population has remained stable and how the average age of the population is steadily rising (see table 4).

SECTORS OF ACTIVITY

Rural areas

In certain rural areas the number of young workers is higher than the national average. These areas are characterised by labour-intensive agriculture and by their great need for labour during the harvest season. Since this kind of activity is often linked with the existence of subfamily or family farms, which are generally but little mechanised, it is indispensable to have recourse to family labour, including child labour, for some jobs.

In a series of special inquiries [7] carried out between 1970 and 1974 it was observed that 39 per cent of the 6- to 9-year-old children, 88 per cent of those aged between 10 and 13 years and 100 per cent of those aged between 14 and 17 years were working on the cotton plantations of the Chaco. These plantations are of four types : (a) small, specialising in cotton production alone ; (b) medium-sized, specialising in cotton production alone ; (c) medium-sized, with diversified production and (d) large, generally with diversified production. They employ child labour in a manner which is consistent within each type. Thus, on type (a) and (b) plantations the proportion of 6- to 9-year-old children employed is 67 and 57 per cent respectively, whereas no children in this age-group work on plantations of types (c) and (d). As regards 10- to 13-year-old children, 100 per cent of those in this age-group are employed on type (a) and (b) plantations as against 75 per cent on type (c) plantations and 67 per cent on type (d) plantations. In this last type there was a tendency for fewer children to be employed the more profitable the plantation was. Nevertheless, on all four types of plantation all the young people between 14 and 17 years of age are to be found at work. The only difference is that, whilst some youngsters on type *(a)* plantations work on rural jobs calling for little skill (clearing ground, cotton picking, etc.), those in the same age-group on type *(d)* plantations take on higher-skilled wage-earning jobs (driving mechanical harvesters, ploughing and preparing land for sowing, etc.) or stable and remunerative employment (e.g. working in the co-operative).

In the tobacco-growing area of Corrientes 31 per cent of the children in the 6 to 9 age-group, 75 per cent of those in the 10 to 13 age-group and 97 per cent of those in the 14 to 17 age-group work on the plantations. In other words, just as in the cotton-growing area, virtually all children are at work from the age of 14 onwards. As above, the plantations may be broken down into four types : *(a)* small subfamily plots (up to 5 hectares) with a high proportion of tenant farmers ; *(b)* larger subfamily plots (6 to 10 hectares) with a greater proportion of owner-farmers ; *(c)* family undertakings ; and *(d)* undertakings whose size permits a typically entrepreneurial development. The smaller the plantation, the greater the number of 6- to 9-year-old children employed on it : thus, whilst on type *(d)* plantations we find 25 per cent of the children in this age-group, on those in type *(a)* there are 50 per cent. There are no significant differences by type of plantation in the other age-groups.

In the case of the small *maté* producers of Misiones, the inquiry was limited to one age-group, and it was found that 29 per cent of the children between the ages of 6 and 13 were working on the farm. This percentage is relatively low because of the method of cultivation, which calls for only a relatively short period of maintenance each year. The *maté* is harvested by teams of migrant workers (usually Paraguayans) who, in many cases, are helped by their families. Practically half the children in the 8 to 15 age-group collaborate with the reapers. From 16 years of age onwards, however, the proportion rises to the region of 100 per cent, although one should note the existence of many solitary reapers, from the age of 16, who do not normally live with their families.

In the same province the proportion of children working on the plantations is much higher in the areas where crops other than *maté* predominate —tea, soya, tobacco, and so on. The picking of tea by hand, for instance, is an activity which (although we have no exact statistics thereon) occupies a large number of children from the ages of 5 or 6. Tea picking is organised on a family basis, often with the help of the children of neighbours, who are subsequently themselves helped in the same way.

In Salta and Jujuy tobacco is grown on medium-sized and large plantations. On the medium-sized plantations the need for labour is usually met through an arrangement under which the owner of the plantation contributes his land and capital and an "associate" is responsible for providing all the manpower needed, in return for a percentage of the production. Consequently, the "associate" uses family labour to the largest extent possible, since he thereby avoids the expense of hiring wage earners ; the inevitable result is a considerable use of young child labour. In the 6 to 9 age-group the proportion of children employed is already 66 per cent, rising to 82 per cent for the 10- to 11-year-olds, whilst from the age of 12 practically all the members of the family are working on the plantation.

The *zafreros* (sugar harvest workers) are paid according to the amount of cane they cut. The members of the family help in the tasks of stripping and loading the cane cut by the *zafrero,* thus increasing output. At other times the women and children prepare the food—a very useful and necessary task, since the *zafrero* works 10 or 12 hours a day, from sunrise to sunset, and must eat his meals out on the plantations. [8]

In the province of Santiago del Estero (for which estimates with the same degree of accuracy are not available), children help with the cotton picking from the age of 5 or 6, and subsequently with the melon and watermelon harvests and with binding alfalfa into sheaves. From the age of 10 onwards they help in practically all the activities of the farm. The children of those employed in stockbreeding look after the livestock, milk the cows and do other jobs about the farm from an early age.

In a valley of the province of Catamarca [9] child labour is employed intensively on growing paprika. Here the mutual sharing of labour is widespread. The grower whose children are of school age sets them to work with the children of his relatives, neighbours, friends—indeed, anyone who will subsequently be able to repay the help given by his own children in this way. Until they are about 15 years old they are mainly engaged on transplanting. When we realise how many small growers there are, we can see how widespread this practice is. Child workers also undertake other jobs on the plantation, mainly weeding.

Urban areas

We have limited our analysis of the use of child labour in urban areas to Greater Buenos Aires, where we contacted a number of key personnel (social assistants in public bodies responsible for child protection, and private (religious) social service organisations which help young people) concerned with the situation of those less than 14 years old.

At present, domestic service is the most common occupation for women of all ages, followed by street trading for the younger girls. Boys carry out a wide range of activities, which may be grouped into four main categories : helping their parents in small family businesses ; street trading ; various service activities ; and (more and more, as they grow older) work in productive establishments in the formal sector.

In fact, there is a greater range of jobs available for boys, including the usual street trades such as cleaning shoes, selling various goods, opening taxi doors, etc. The building industry, especially at the informal level, maintains a pool of children who have been recruited directly through parents, relatives or friends. In the commercial sector—in bars and bakeries, for instance—children are employed to clean up, often late at night.

Children are also recruited for the services sector ; in general, these children come from better off families and are still at school. They work as messengers, delivery boys, and so on.

EDUCATION AND VOCATIONAL TRAINING

A good number of children leave school at the end of the primary stage. About 50 per cent do so before reaching that stage. Those who get a job which requires a period of apprenticeship are in effect trained at the work-place ; in the case of the most flagrant examples of the exploitation of child workers that we mentioned above (children employed on unskilled agricultural jobs and as urban street traders), there is no form of apprenticeship that could help the child to get a better job at a later date.

In a study on school drop-outs in Argentina, published in 1964, a number of suggestions were put forward in an attempt to explain why children leave school early. The reasons for the high proportion of drop-outs all seem to be connected with the problem of child labour, for example "population has no fixed roots", "family continuously on the move in search of work", "family has no permanent base". Migration of this kind, which has long been known in Argentina by the name "swallow" migration, considerably hampers any continuity in a child's schooling, particularly when the school calendar clashes with certain agricultural activities. An associated reason is perhaps the very early entry of rural children into the active labour force, which is made possible by the simple nature of some rural jobs, such as clearing ground. On a more general plane, these cases would be covered by the following proposition : the lower the socio-economic level of the family, the greater the need to make economic use of the children, despite the legal restrictions involved. It is thus inevitable that the continuity of the children's studies is adversely affected. [10]

There is a steady increase in the number of children who stay on at school, at both the national and the provincial levels. The percentage of children who do stay on is lowest, however, in rural areas, particularly in the rural areas of certain provinces. We may therefore say that the problem of school drop-outs is largely a rural phenomenon, since when a child is recruited into the labour force it is virtually impossible for him to continue his studies.

Notes

[1] GDP per head in purchasers' values, 1975 (United Nations : *Monthly Bulletin of Statistics* (New York), June 1978).

[2] 1955-61 figures, from Jorge Somoza : *La mortalidad en la Argentina entre 1869 y 1960* (Buenos Aires, Ediciones del Instituto, 1971).

[3] Zulma Recchini de Lattes and Alfredo E. Lattes (compilers) : *La población de la Argentina* (Buenos Aires, INDEC, 1975), p. 34.

[4] Floreal Forni : "Familia y sociedad rural en la Argentina", in *Investigaciones en sociología* (Mendoza, National University of Cuyo, 1965).

[5] Raúl Bisio and Floreal Forni : *Empleo rural en la República Argentina 1937-1969*, Working paper no. 1 (Buenos Aires, CEIL, 1977) ; María Isabel Tort and Nora Mendizábal : *Evolución de la tecnología agropecuaria y su relación con el uso de mano de obra* (Buenos Aires, CEIL, 1977 ; unpublished).

[6] Lattes and Lattes, op. cit., p. 72.

[7] This information has been made available to us by the National Directorate of Rural Economy and Sociology of the State Secretariat of Agriculture and Stockbreeding.

[8] Raúl Bisio and Floreal Forni : "Economía de enclave y satelización del mercado de trabajo rural : El caso de los trabajadores con empleo precario en un ingenio azucarero del noroeste argentino", in *Desarrollo Económico : Revista de Ciencias Sociales* (Buenos Aires), Apr.-June 1976.

[9] Carlos A. Herrán : *Migraciones y estructura social en el valle de Santa María, Pcia. de Catamarca* (National University of Misiones, Faculty of Social Sciences, Social Research Centre, 1976).

[10] CFI : *La deserción escolar en la Argentina* (Buenos Aires, 1964), p. 21.

GREECE

Theodora Papaflessa * and Sophia Spiliotopoulos **

9

SOCIOCULTURAL BACKGROUND

The position of the child in Greek society—notwithstanding the fact that this is a society which is in the process of transition from a rural to an urban way of life—is still determined primarily by the important role played by the extended family and by the value accorded to family ties. A second influence on the sociocultural life of the Greek child is the educational system, which is moving towards a system designed to meet the needs of a modern industrial society, at the expense of the old, purely humanistic approach.

SOME DATA ON POPULATION

Table 5 gives information on the composition of the population by broad age-group during the third quarter of the present century, and reveals trends towards a lower birth rate, lower population growth and higher life expectancy.

Migration, both internal and external, has had a considerable impact on the disproportionate ageing and underpopulation of certain areas ; internal migration to Athens and Salonika (where 64 per cent of the urban population is concentrated) will probably continue.

SECTORS OF ACTIVITY

Table 6 gives data on the distribution of the economically active population by branch of economic activity. Boys constitute 1.24 per cent of the total economically active population and 1.72 per cent of the male economically active population. The corresponding proportions for girls are 0.77 per cent and 2.75 per cent.

---

* Social worker ; Assistant Director, YWCA School of Social Work, Athens.
** Attorney-at-law, Athens.

Children at work

Table 5.   Greece : population by age-group, 1951, 1961, 1971, 1975

Age-group	1951		1961		1971		1975 (mid-year estimates)	
	No.	%	No.	%	No.	%	No.	%
Up to 14	2 165 966	28	2 243 962	27	2 223 904	25	2 160 453	24
(10-14	778 065	10	732 891	9	724 732	8	—	—)
15-64	4 945 583	65	5 457 937	65	5 587 352	64	5 779 392	64
65 and above	521 252	7	686 654	8	957 116	11	1 106 692	12
Total	7 632 801	100	8 388 553	100	8 768 372	100	9 046 542	100

Source. National Statistical Service.

Unofficial information provided mainly by social workers shows that many children are hired by small undertakings and workshops for short periods of time and are then dismissed before they become eligible for social insurance or are registered with the Labour Inspection Office. It is unlikely that these children are listed in any of the official statistics.

Children below the age of 14 are probably hired on the same short-term basis, and again are probably not known to the labour inspection services.

The children listed by the National Statistical Service as "self-employed" may well be those who work as street traders or who do piece-work at home. Public opinion in this matter may be said to be divided between those who consider these children to be industrious and worthy of praise and those who believe that the irregular hours and the conditions under which they work do more harm than good.

Although statistics on employment in rural areas are not yet available, it seems that children work beside their parents in all agricultural undertakings. This type of work is considered to be legitimate and justifiable as a contribution to the family's well-being. It is a seasonal activity and the degree of intensity depends on the type of crop : for example, in tobacco-growing areas long hours and long periods of work are called for. In most instances the main demand for seasonal labour in rural areas coincides with the school holidays.

More and more children are employed during the school holidays to help their parents in small shops, hotels, restaurants, and so on. Their remuneration and working conditions vary widely. As the school holidays last for three months, there is time both for play and for productive employment. Again, many unskilled jobs are available during the summer, as for example in the main tourist areas.

There seems to be some justification for saying that the proportion of child employment is declining, since the respective percentages for boys and girls in the labour force over the past two decades are as follows : 1961, 20.3

Table 6. Greece : economically active population by sector of activity, area and age-group

Sector of activity	Urban areas		Semi-urban areas		Rural areas		All areas		% distribution of child labour force by sector
	10-65 years	10-14 years	10-65 years	10-14 years	10-65 years	10-14 years	10-65 years	10-14 years	
Agriculture, livestock, etc.	83 416	1 024	174 424	4 024	1 054 760	30 348	1 312 600	35 396	54.36
Mining, quarrying, saltworks	5 364	4	4 683	40	11 044	156	21 096	200	0.30
Manufacturing	439 400	10 152	50 016	2 020	64 964	4 092	554 390	16 264	24.98
Electricity, gas, water supply, etc.	19 328	16	2 540	4	2 948	12	24 816	32	0.05
Construction, public works	172 440	2 456	31 943	728	52 036	1 152	256 424	4 336	6.66
Trade, restaurants, hotels	275 724	3 212	37 140	656	49 160	1 004	362 024	4 872	7.48
Transports, storage, communications	160 436	124	22 716	40	28 520	120	211 672	284	0.44
Banking, insurance, real estate	71 464	128	4 424	4	2 636	4	78 524	136	0.21
Services	262 572	964	33 840	128	52 692	224	349 104	1 316	2.02
Not declared	53 156	1 676	4 092	200	7 108	400	64 356	2 276	3.50
Total	1 543 300	19 756	365 828	7 844	1 325 868	37 512	3 234 996	65 112	100.00

Source. National Statistical Service : Statistical Yearbook of Greece 1977 (Athens, 1978).

and 16.0 per cent ; 1971, 10.3 and 7.1 per cent ; 1975 (estimated), 7 and 5 per cent ; and 1980 (estimated), 3 and 2 per cent. The estimates for 1975 and 1980 would seem to be fair, since the period of compulsory education is being extended to nine years and, moreover, the introduction of vocational training classes will do away with apprenticeship to a large extent.

It is noticeable that the odd jobs that in the past were done by young children—such as delivering goods—are more and more being undertaken by youths or adults. Again, the old practice of hiring very young girls for domestic service has now almost completely died out.

It seems that the majority of young persons and children employed as wage earners work in manufacturing, usually in small-scale and cottage industries. These small undertakings are found mainly in or around the large urban areas.

WORKING CONDITIONS AND ENVIRONMENT

Many of the small undertakings in which the majority of young wage earners work operate in rather dubious conditions of safety and health, with inadequately guarded machinery. Frequent accidents are the result. Because of the limited number of inspectors, and because these undertakings are scattered over large areas and may only operate for a short time, it is not possible for them to be inspected regularly. The manager of one of these undertakings may or may not announce to the authorities that the undertaking is operative or submit personnel lists, and it may therefore be that they employ children and young persons without observing the legislation.

As the minimum age for employment in hotels and restaurants is 12 years, it is obvious that children as young as this are exposed to both physical and moral danger. Even if the hotel or restaurant is a family concern, work therein may be prejudicial to the child's health if the working conditions are poor, or if the hours of employment are long, and so on. Although children who have not yet completed primary school are legally not allowed to work in this sector, there is some reason to believe that this prohibition is not respected. Even where parents want their children to attend school as long as possible, perhaps beyond the period of compulsory education, the fact that the school holidays coincide with the high tourist season implies intensive work and late hours for children working in this sector (in summer, restaurants and similar establishments stay open until well after midnight).

The construction industry is one of the most hazardous for young people (and for adult workers too), even though it is well covered by safety and health legislation.

Conditions of work in family businesses in general vary widely. Of course, the children are generally in less moral danger than elsewhere, but it cannot be said that there are no physical dangers, as the parents themselves often do not recognise occupational hazards and, since the undertaking is usually small, safety measures are often not observed.

The authorities no longer issue permits to children selling articles in the streets or in public places. It is therefore not possible to tell how many children are engaged in this type of activity, but it seems that their number has decreased to some extent. However, the moral and physical hazards that are part and parcel of street trading are perhaps greater than before, especially in urban areas (traffic, air pollution, and so on).

A practice that is common in certain trades (e.g. shoemaking, tailoring) is the employment of "workers' assistants", when the worker hires someone to help him to do his job. This assistant (usually a younger person or a child) works under the direct supervision of the worker (or craftsman in charge) but also under the higher supervision of the employer, with whom he has an indirect relationship. Members of the worker's family may be employed as assistants. The question whether a particular person is in fact a worker's assistant is often difficult to answer. There are cases where the engagement of an assistant is used as a cover when the law is being broken.

The provisions regarding maximum hours of work apply in principle to all workers, irrespective of age. Since 1 July 1978 maximum working hours in industrial and non-industrial occupations have in principle been eight hours per day and 45 hours per week. In theory, employers are not allowed to give young persons under 18 who have completed their daily working hours any work to be done, either for the employer or for a third person, outside the place of employment. Overtime and nightwork permits are not granted to children.

REMUNERATION

In both industrial and non-industrial employment remuneration varies according to age. The present minimum wages for children are as follows : (a) minimum monthly wage of non-manual workers—young persons between the ages of 14 and 16 receive 71.42 per cent of the adult minimum wage for the job ; and (b) minimum daily wage of manual workers—apprentices under 18 years of age receive from 65 per cent to 85 per cent of the adult minimum wage for the job, depending on the length of time they have worked for the same employer.

Collective agreements covering particular sectors of employment or particular professions also provide for lower wages for young persons. These can vary from 60 to 90 per cent of the adult minimum wage, depending on the type of job, number of years of service, qualifications, and so on.

DURATION OF EMPLOYMENT

The available statistics show the duration of employment by sector of activity but not by age-group. It is therefore difficult to state whether children work permanently, at irregular intervals or seasonally. It seems, however, that most children work at irregular intervals and seasonally. This is because employers tend to employ children for a short period of time in order to evade certain responsibilities, and because a number of jobs are seasonal in nature (e.g. work connected with the tourist industry, work in the agricultural products industries, work in agriculture).

EDUCATION AND VOCATIONAL TRAINING

A new educational system was introduced in 1977, but to date there is little information to hand about its results. Primary schooling is compulsory for a period of six years, and the normal school-leaving age is between 11 and 12 years, which corresponds approximately to the legal minimum age for admission to non-industrial (excluding agricultural) employment (12 years). Children aged 14 years who have not completed their primary education can continue at day school ; otherwise they are obliged to attend a night school, provided that there is one in the area in which they live.

Secondary education is at present in a state of transition, as a result of the planned raising of the period of compulsory schooling to nine years, with a consequent raising of the normal school-leaving age to between 14 and 15 years. As part of the reform of the existing school system, from 1980 onwards vocational training will be provided by vocational high schools or by a new type of vocational secondary school.

On-the-job training is at present provided only by the Manpower Employment Organisation, which places pupils in undertakings where they work as apprentices during their studies ; they are paid a percentage of the minimum adult wage, which increases every term and is between 20 and 90 per cent of the adult wage. The proportion of pupil-apprentices to the number of workers employed is fixed by the Ministry of Labour and varies between one to ten and one to three. Pupil-apprentices up to 17 years of age are allowed by law to work one hour less than normal working hours. The Labour Inspection Office and the educational authorities require that working children attending any kind of vocational or general education night school should work the same shorter hours. Those up to 25 years of age who work in commerce may also leave work one hour before the evening closing time, so as to attend vocational night schools.

LEGISLATION

The legislation in force concerning child labour and the conditions under which children work is highly complex. It is scattered over various instruments, both outdated and modern, at various levels. Several attempts made to codify all labour legislation have not been successful, due to the inadequate administrative framework and to the need for constant adaptation to changing needs.

Turning to the main sectors of activity in which children work, we note that there is no special legal protection of children and young persons working in agriculture (indeed, Greece has no special legislation concerning the conditions of work and employment in this sector). In industrial and non-industrial (except agricultural) occupations, the basic labour provisions on the employment and work of children and young persons are Law No. 4029 of 1912 on the employment of women and children and the decrees enacted in application thereof, as well as the provisions concerning children and young persons included in some later labour laws. The minimum age for admission to employment in public or private industrial undertakings and branches thereof is 14 years, except for employment in family undertakings or work in technical schools which are approved and supervised by the public authority. The employment of children and young persons in hazardous occupations is subject to further restrictions. With regard to non-industrial employment, the minimum age at which children may begin work is in principle 12 years for workers or apprentices in commercial undertakings, restaurants and hotels. Children under 14 years old are prohibited from selling any articles on the street, in theatres and in other places of public entertainment, and from working in domestic service in private households. Persons under 15 years of age are not allowed to work on board ships of any kind, except for ships on board which only members of the same family are employed, where the minimum age is reduced to 14 years.

Greece has ratified the ILO Night Work of Young Persons (Industry) Convention (Revised), 1948, under which with certain exceptions night work by young persons under 18 years of age in industry is prohibited. Night work in non-industrial employment is prohibited for young persons under 18 in commercial undertakings and under 14 in restaurants and hotels. No person under 16 years of age may sell articles on the street after 9 p.m. and before 5 a.m. (except for boy newspaper-sellers over 12 years of age).

Work on Sundays and legal holidays is generally prohibited for persons under 16 years of age in industrial undertakings and in commercial establishments.

Workers under 18 years of age are entitled to annual paid leave of at least 18 consecutive working days.

Other legal provisions relate to the maximum weight to be carried by young people and to pre-employment medical examinations.

In general, family undertakings are usually excluded from protective labour legislation.

LABOUR INSPECTION

Hitherto, the number of labour inspectors seems always to be been inadequate for the duties the labour inspection service has to fulfil. However, in the very near future their numbers are to be increased by more than

50 per cent, and it may thus be expected that the admitted inefficiencies of the past may not be repeated. Even so, the large number of small undertakings scattered throughout the country will continue to make the inspectors' task a formidable one.

INDIA

K. D. Gangrade *

10

SOCIOCULTURAL BACKGROUND

In traditional India no family unit is considered complete without children, and the feeling of corporate responsibility of family members towards dependants of all types ensures that care and protection is extended to youngsters in need. The problem of child labour in India may seem to result from traditional attitudes, urbanisation, industrialisation, migration, a lack of schools or the reluctance of parents to send their children to school, and so on ; however, its main causes are extreme poverty and the fact that agriculture is the main occupation of the majority of the population.

The poverty of many families forces the parents to put their children to work instead of sending them to school. Children often need their meagre wages so badly that they corroborate the false statements made by their employer about their age, to evade the supervision of the labour inspectorate. The position is so serious that protective measures, such as the prohibition of employment below a certain age, are not always strictly enforced, for fear that the children will be driven to live by thieving.

In some families, when disease or other forms of disability upset the delicate balance of the family budget, there may be no alternative but to send the children to work. If the child's education suffers in the process, it is the poverty of the parents which is to be blamed. A large majority of rural and slum dwellers cannot afford to educate their children, though education is free up to primary level. For them, uneducated children are an asset, and the desire to educate them becomes a double liability because of, first, the loss of earnings of the child who does not work, and second, the expenditure involved in education, however low it may be. In rural families especially, the economics of using school-age children for agricultural work weigh heavily against sending them to school and keeping them in school.

The other obvious reasons for employing child labour are that it is very cheap and that it is readily available in the agricultural and rural sectors. In

---

* Vice-Principal, Delhi School of Social Work, University of Delhi.

plantations the family works as a group : the parents do the main work and the children help them by plucking the tea leaves or the coffee berries or by collecting latex, or they do the secondary jobs such as weeding, spreading fertiliser, and so on.

SOME DATA ON POPULATION

According to the 1971 national population census, there are 228 million children less than 14 years of age in India, out of a total population of 548 million. This figure represents 42 per cent of the whole. Of these children, 186 million live in rural areas, 115 million are less than 6 years old and 113 million are between 7 and 14 years old.

AGE OF WORKING CHILDREN

Data relating to the age at which children begin to work are not readily available from the census. However, individual surveys have shown that the age of entry varies according to the place and the occupation : children only 6 years old have been found working, although the usual age of entry into employment seems to be 8 to 9 years. Boys of 10 to 12 have been found working on regular term contracts of several years duration. A study of child labour in Bombay revealed that 24.7 per cent of working children began work between the ages of 6 and 9, 48.4 per cent between the ages of 10 and 12 and 26.9 per cent between the ages of 13 and 15. [1] In other words, one working child in every four was below the age of 9 years when he joined the labour force.

According to the 1971 national population census, the total number of child workers (i.e. children less than 15 years of age) was 10.7 million, representing 4.7 per cent of the total child population and 5.9 per cent of the total labour force. Of these, about 7.9 million were boys and 2.8 million girls. It should be mentioned that between 1961 and 1971 the number of children at work fell from 14.5 million to 10.7 million.

SECTORS OF ACTIVITY

As table 7 shows, most child workers in India are employed in agriculture.

There have been no surveys to determine what proportion of working children are self-employed, gainfully employed, or unpaid. However, in agricultural family undertakings child workers are generally unpaid. According to the National Sample Survey, the proportion of unpaid family workers in rural India amounted to some 15 to 17 per cent of the male labour force and to between 41 and 49 per cent of the female labour force. The propor-

Table 7. India : child labour (age 0-14) by sex and sector of activity, 1971
(Thousands)

Activity	Boys	Girls
Cultivators	3 125	746
Agricultural labourers	3 004	1 582
Forestry and plantations	744	142
Mining and quarrying	14	9
Manufacturing	440	214
Construction	42	17
Trade and commerce	198	14
Transport	36	6
Others	282	123
Total	7 885	2 853

Source. Office of the Registrar-General of the Census : *Census report 1971.*

tion of unpaid family workers aged 10 and over, estimated from the 1961 census, was about 14 per cent for males and 41 per cent for females. It is therefore clear that the proportion of unpaid female workers is much higher than that of unpaid male workers and that they form an important part of the labour force.

As regards the distribution of jobs between the sexes, there seems to be no particular division of labour between men, women and children in agricultural family undertakings, although the pattern of women's participation shows regional and cultural variations.

As regards the work done by children, the girls look after their younger brothers and sisters, cook meals and do various other odd jobs in the house. This type of work is rarely undertaken by boys. In domestic jobs and in construction labour the girls outnumber the boys. Boys generally do jobs such as cleaning shoes, pulling rickshaws, selling newspapers, working in car workshops and garages, and so on.

WORKING CONDITIONS AND ENVIRONMENT

Though data are very scanty here, they do give some idea of the situation in certain sectors of activity. Studies carried out in Delhi, [2] Madras [3] and Bombay [4] and the study made by the Labour Bureau of the Ministry of Labour [5] give a harrowing picture of the working conditions and environment in which children have to live and work. The tea stalls and *dhabas* (roadside cafés) where children work are generally situated in the busy areas of cities. They are often small (sometimes only 1.5 by 2 metres), with uneven floors and rickety walls and roofs. Children working at these places are exposed to the vagaries of the weather, since they mostly have to work in the open without adequate clothing or footwear. When they live on the premises, conditions are equally bad : they sleep either in the kitchen or on an open veranda.

The most unhygienic working conditions are those endured by the children who collect rags and other waste materials. Even a casual look at their physique and clothing reveals the extent of their poverty and deprivation ; even in the most severe winter, they can be seen working in the open without a single sweater or other protective clothing.

The Labour Bureau found that in small-scale and cottage industries (such as watch manufacture, cashew-nut processing, carpet manufacture, and so on) the employment of under-age children is still common. The number of hours worked was found to be in excess of the legal maximum ; in cottage industries, children were obliged to work as long as adult workers, except where the home work system was prevalent. The working conditions for children in the glass industry continue to be deplorable. By far the greater number of child workers work more than six hours a day. In establishments not covered by the law, exploitation is likely to be considerable. Children in unlicensed *dhabas* and tea stalls often work more than ten hours a day. The picture as regards domestic service is much the same : children usually work between nine and ten hours a day throughout the year, with a one-hour break between 1 p.m. and 2 p.m.

An inquiry concerning children under 12 years of age working on plantations showed that 25.6 per cent of the children were in an advanced stage of vitamin A deficiency. One in ten of the children showed sign of riboflavin deficiency. Anaemia and chronic bronchitis are common among child workers in the *bidi* (local cigarettes) industry.

REMUNERATION

Child workers, particularly in rural areas, are paid both in cash and in kind (food, clothes, accommodation, etc.). Although statistics are rather sketchy, it appears that as a general rule children receive approximately one-half the adult wage, although the rate is frequently less than the legal minimum. In the *bidi,* match and mica industries in particular, children's wages are much lower than those of adults. Child workers generally pay a large part of their earnings to their parents, retaining only a small amount for their personal expenditure.

EDUCATION AND VOCATIONAL TRAINING

During the past quarter-of-a-century the enrolment in school of children in the 6 to 10 age-group has risen from 42.6 to 82.7 per cent and in the 11 to 14 age-group from 12.7 to 36 per cent. Despite the various efforts made under successive Five-Year Plans, the education of girls is still a serious problem, with enrolments of 38.9, 31.8 and 28.2 per cent in the primary, middle and secondary schools respectively. In 1971 the literacy rate for men and women was 39.5 and 18.7 per cent respectively ; but despite the increase that this represents over the 1951 figure, because of rapid population growth the absolute number of illiterates rose from 213 million to 387 million over the same period.

There is a high drop-out rate between the primary and middle school stages (73 per cent of boys and 80 per cent of girls) and a somewhat lower rate between the middle and secondary school stages (45 per cent of boys and 52 per cent of girls). It has been estimated that well over half of these drop-outs are the result of abject poverty and other economic reasons that force the child to go out to earn a living.

Vocational training institutions for children are virtually non-existent, and most children learn their job whilst at work. Some training is provided by the All India Handicrafts Board and by Bal-Sahyog (a voluntary child welfare agency).

LEGISLATION

Under article 29 of the Constitution no child below the age of 14 years is to be employed on work in any factory or mine or engaged in any other hazardous employment. The main instrument relating to the exploitation of child labour is the Factories Act of 1948, which extends to the whole of India and applies to establishments employing ten or more workers working with the aid of power or 20 or more working without the aid of power. It provides, inter alia, for the medical examination of young workers between the ages of 15 and 18. Various other Acts relating to specific sectors of activity (mining, plantations, merchant shipping, motor transport, commercial undertakings, etc.) have also clarified the position of children working in these sectors, and their wages are regulated by the Minimum Wages Act of 1948.

The usefulness and importance of this legislation lies in the fact that it lays down the age limits and hours of work for the employment of children. The Acts also provide safeguards for the health and conditions of work of the workers. They have their limitations, however, in that they are applicable only to duly registered undertakings. As 42.7 per cent of child workers are employed in the informal and agricultural sectors, the enforcement of these Acts is not easy.

Notes

[1] Singh, Kaura and Khan : *Working children in Bombay : A study,* op. cit., table 45.

[2] *Working children in urban Delhi : A research report by the Indian Council for Child Welfare* (New Delhi, 1977).

[3] K. N. George : *Child labour in the city of Madras,* paper presented to the National Seminar on the Employment of Children in India organised by the National Institute of Public Co-operation and Child Development, New Delhi, Aug. 1977.

[4] Singh, Kaura and Khan : *Working children in Bombay : A study,* op. cit.

[5] Ministry of Labour, Labour Bureau : *Child labour in India* (Simla, 1954).

INDONESIA

F. Soeratno *

11

SOCIOCULTURAL BACKGROUND

In Indonesia by far the most common family pattern is the extended family, and the resulting close relationship between the members of a family has a strong influence on the children's development. Tradition still plays a leading role in the life of a child, in particular with regard to his obligations towards and relations with the parents and other relatives.

SOME DATA ON POPULATION

According to the 1971 national population census, 53.6 per cent of the population of Indonesia were less than 19 years old. The average population growth rate between 1961 and 1971 was just over 2 per cent. Although 82 per cent of the population live in rural areas and only 18 per cent in the towns, the growth rate of a number of cities in recent years has been phenomenal. For instance, the annual growth rate of Jakarta seems to have been about 4.5 per cent for the past few decades, and the population rose from 2.9 million in 1961 to over 4.5 million in 1971.

The Indonesian labour force amounts to 36 per cent of the total population—a lower figure than in most other Asian countries. The percentage of children in this labour force is shown in table 8.

AGE OF WORKING CHILDREN
AND SECTORS OF ACTIVITY

· The traditional principle of mutual assistance which operates in rural areas influences the age at which children begin work. When it is seen that a local child is in poor circumstances or needs help, it often happens that he is "adopted" by another family to help in the family business, usually

---

* Lawyer ; member of the National Council of Social Welfare, Jakarta.

Table 8. Indonesia : estimated child labour force by age-group and sex, as a percentage of the total population over 10 years of age

Age-group	Boys			Girls		
	Urban	Rural	Total	Urban	Rural	Total
10-14	7.6	25.5	22.6	5.8	17.5	15.6
15-19	45.8	71.6	66.7	24.2	32.0	30.6

without any regularly paid money wage. The child performs services which are generally looked upon as a servant's tasks. There is obviously no particular minimum age at which this "adoption" occurs, but usually it is higher than 8 or 9 years.

In some rural areas where mutual assistance is common, wages are paid in kind and only boys who are almost 14 years old are "adopted". The type of work done under such arrangements includes house building, agricultural jobs, and so on.

In Jakarta and other cities, children under 9 years of age are found working in the services sector—for instance, as shoeblacks or selling cigarettes and newspapers. Older boys sell ceramics, food, drinks, etc., and older girls sell medicine, drinks, rice, etc. These goods are usually prepared by the parents.

In small-scale industry, labour is usually recruited through personal contacts and (as in rural areas) generally according to mutual assistance principles. The usual age for recruitment is 14 years, and mainly girls are engaged.

Such statistics as exist on the number of children employed are not very reliable, but it is felt by employers and parents alike that the number is declining.

On the outer islands of the Indonesian archipelago (other than Java) children are employed on plantations, which were formerly run by foreigners but which have now been taken over by the Government.

Where the parents are wage earners or homeworkers (as occurs in the cigarette industry, for instance) they are often helped by their children.

In the manufacturing sector children work in cigarette and tobacco factories, in the textile and handicrafts industries (e.g. batik) and in other small-scale industries. For several reasons, however, such as the need to escape the attentions of the labour inspection services, many children carry out their work not in the factory itself but at home.

Indonesian children carry out the usual informal sector activities on the streets of the big cities, generally on their own account.

Although their numbers are diminishing, family undertakings employing child labour are still in existence. They survive particularly outside the big cities, in areas where society is basically traditional in outlook.

WORKING CONDITIONS AND ENVIRONMENT

In family undertakings wages are usually paid in kind (food, lodging, clothes). In these undertakings, for reasons of tradition, there is something of a family relationship rather than an employer-worker relationship and, although working hours for the family are not restricted, those of the hired worker are limited to seven hours a day.

In some factories where the employment relationship is governed by a contract the stipulated period of work is often not observed. It thus happens that in the cigarette industry the girls work from 5 a.m. until 5 p.m., with a break of one hour at midday. It is said that this arrangement is voluntary.

REMUNERATION

Wage-earning children are sometimes paid annually or at intervals of several months. It should be mentioned that the wages of children performing the same work as an adult are usually about 70 or 80 per cent of the adult wage.

With regard to annual leave, those employed on a regular basis are sometimes entitled to one month's leave during the period of Ramadan and sometimes for two weeks after that (the Idulfitri feast). Workers are also sometimes released to help with the harvest at home. Whether this leave is awarded or not depends on the quality of the harvest and its nature (irregular or seasonal).

There seem to be no effective regulations regarding annual holidays. Consequently, many of the children employed take their own decisions with regard to their free time. In family businesses in the cities the children are usually allowed two weeks holiday so that they can fulfil their obligations to visit the cemetery and their parents in their home villages.

EDUCATION AND VOCATIONAL TRAINING

Officially, attendance at school is compulsory. If, however, as is often the case, there is no school for a child to go to, it is obvious that this requirement cannot be fulfilled. In fact, parents do not send their children to work because they are reluctant to send them to school but rather because of the shortage of schools. Many communities have established "community classes", which are intended for children who have finished their primary schooling and who are not able to continue with their education at a general or vocational secondary school. These classes have a vocational slant, so that the children learn about agriculture, fishery, co-operatives, and so on.

Table 9 shows the educational levels reached by the population over 10 years of age in 1971.

Table 9.   Indonesia : population aged 10 years and above by level
of educational attainment, 1971

Level of educational attainment	Urban		Rural		Total
	Male	Female	Male	Female	
School not attended	12.4	31.4	33.8	56.0	41.0
Primary school not completed	30.1	29.2	39.2	28.6	33.0
Primary school	30.8	23.7	13.6	13.6	19.4
General junior secondary school	10.8	7.8	2.5	1.1	3.1
Vocational junior secondary school	6.6	3.0	0.6	0.1	1.2
General senior secondary school	3.6	2.1	1.1	0.4	1.1
Vocational senior secondary school	3.4	2.1	0.0	0.2	0.9
Academy	1.2	0.4	—	—	0.2
University	1.1	0.3	—	—	0.1
Total	100.0	100.0	100.0	100.0	100.0

The skill training centres established by the Ministry of Manpower were
set up for those working for small-scale employers, who would be unable to
provide such training on their own account. The orientation of the courses
held in the centres is essentially practical.

Vocational on-the-job training is less developed ; indeed, there is still
a general preference for employing children for a limited number of hours
per day, so that they may spend the rest of the day receiving general education or vocational training in educational establishments.

LEGISLATION

An apparent loophole in Law No. 14 of 1969 (Basic Provisions respecting
Manpower) has been used by some employers to justify the use of child
labour, notwithstanding the fact that Law No. 1 of 1951 (to Bring the Labour
Law No. 12 of 1948 into Operation throughout Indonesia) prohibits the
employment of children of 14 years of age or younger. To strengthen the
enforcement of this law (mostly in small-scale industries and traditional
undertakings), it is also laid down that "if a child of 6 years or older is found
in an enclosed place where work is being carried on, the child shall be
deemed to be unlawfully employed on work unless the contrary is evident".
The Law also provides that young persons (i.e. males or females over the
age of 14 years but under the age of 18 years) shall not be employed on
work at night, nor on work in mines or quarries, nor on work which is
dangerous or injurious to their health.

ITALY

Elías Mendelievich *

12

SOCIOCULTURAL BACKGROUND

The social scene in Italy today is marked by a number of apparent contra-
dictions which have an effect on the social and labour organisation of the
country, including child labour. First, Italy is a country with an advanced
scientific and industrial infrastructure, but this infrastructure does not function to the best advantage. Second, the north of the country is a highly
developed region, whereas the south is much less advanced. Thus, despite
the fact that the political unification of the country took place well over a
century ago, the sociocultural and economic structure and the mentality of
the inhabitants still differ widely from region to region.

Italy is one of the European countries most affected by the present world
economic crisis, and within the country it is the south—the least developed
region—that is bearing the brunt of the recession. Although the scourge of
unemployment is apparent throughout Italy, it is in the south that most of
the unemployed are found, notwithstanding the fact that many unemployed
southern Italians migrate to the north (especially to Lombardy, Piedmont
and Liguria) in search of work. It is also in the south that "black labour" has
expanded to the greatest extent, in small clandestine undertakings that manage largely to evade paying taxes and social security contributions and deliberately ignore minimum-wage regulations and other types of workers' benefits.

These structural factors, linked with the sociocultural factors mentioned
above, lead to a widespread use of child labour in the south of Italy (especially
in Sicily, Calabria, Campania and Puglia) and amongst the children of
migrants from the south who live in the industrialised areas of the north. One
ventures to suggest that if the unemployed adults replaced the clandestine
child workers in the south, the twin problems of adult unemployment and
child labour would be solved at the same time.

In line with the traditional mentality of a sizeable proportion of the population (and by no means only the very poor), children must know how to

---

* International Labour Office, Geneva.

Table 10.   Italy : resident population by age-group and sex, 1 January 1976

Age-group	Male	Female	Total
Up to 4	2 205 020	2 089 033	4 294 053
5- 9	2 316 123	2 201 025	4 517 148
10-14	2 353 249	2 239 179	4 592 428
15-19	2 126 062	2 034 900	4 160 962
20-64	15 511 709	16 047 357	31 559 066
65 and above	2 880 585	4 009 924	6 890 509
Total	27 392 748	28 621 418	56 014 166

Source. Central Statistics Institute : *Popolazione e movimiento anagrafico dei comuni*, Vol. XXI, 1977.

earn their living from an early age and thus contribute to the family income through their work. We may therefore add another contradiction to those mentioned above : on the one hand, the Italians feel and profess a great love of children, yet on the other hand part of the population exploits them harshly whilst the rest accepts this exploitation as if it were the most natural thing in the world.

Boys work in a wide variety of sectors (to be described later), whilst the girls are concentrated above all in small home industries, agriculture and hairdressers' shops.

Although girls and boys usually do different jobs, in Italy today there are approximately as many girls as boys on the labour market.

Most working children have no time to play ; but even those who do have a spare moment are confronted with an acute shortage of recreational facilities.

SOME DATA ON POPULATION

Table 10 shows the total population of Italy on 1 January 1976, broken down by age-group and sex. It will be seen that in Italy, unlike the situation in the developing countries, the proportion of young people as a percentage of the total population is not high ; in fact, the population in the 0 to 14 age-group represents barely one-quarter of the total.

STATISTICS AND ESTIMATES RELATING
TO THE NUMBER OF WORKING CHILDREN

As we have seen, in one section of the population the employment of child labour is traditional, but there are numerous indications that the number of working children has been increasing during the past few years, in direct

Table 11. Italy : total and economically active population by age-group and sex, 1975
(Thousands)

Age-group	Male			Female			Total		
	Total population	Economically active population		Total population	Economically active population		Total population	Economically active population	
		No.	%		No.	%		No.	%
Up to 15	6 728	70	1.0	6 465	44	0.7	13 193	144	0.9
15-19	2 037	1 034	50.8	1 958	719	36.7	3 995	1 753	43.9
20-24	1 943	1 555	80.0	1 890	867	45.9	3 833	2 422	63.2
25-44	7 577	7 237	95.5	7 599	2 497	32.9	15 176	9 734	64.1
45-54	3 448	3 109	90.2	3 695	1 077	29.2	7 143	4 186	58.6
55-64	2 434	1 429	58.7	2 783	391	14.0	5 217	1 819	34.9
65 and above	2 685	376	14.0	3 780	121	3.2	6 466	497	7.7
Total	26 852	14 811	55.2	28 171	5 716	20.3	55 023	20 527	37.3

Source. ILO : *Year Book of Labour Statistics, 1978* (Geneva, 1978).

relationship with the increase of unemployment among adults. If, on the one hand, there are parallel increases in adult unemployment and in child labour, on the other hand the ever-rising numbers of children who attend school should tend to reduce adult unemployment. The final result of the equation seems to be an increase, however. Unfortunately, it is not possible to give exact figures here, as the statistics and estimates on the subject differ widely. For example, the 1978 edition of the ILO *Year Book of Labour Statistics* states that 114,000 children less than 15 years of age were at work in 1975 (see table 11) : the Ministry of Labour and Social Welfare calculated that already by 1971 130,000 children were working illegally ; [1] and a statistical sampling carried out in 1976 by a specialised institute produced a figure of 106,000 children. [2] Notwithstanding these estimates, some authors do not hesitate to put the figure at 500,000 [3] or even 700,000, [4] whilst estimates in Italian newspapers are higher still. In general, observers agree that a considerable proportion of illegal child labour in Italy is concentrated in the Naples region.

An indirect method of calculating the number of working children is to count up the number of children who have left school. This method cannot be exact, however, because very many children are registered as being in school but are very frequently absent. Moreover, it could only be applied to those young people who work full time.

The age at which children begin to work varies according to the region, the type of work, their school results and the attitude of their parents. Generally speaking, the older a child becomes, the more likely he is to be going out to work, and it can be stated that the majority begin to work between the ages of 12 and 15. However, an interesting investigation carried out in Altamura, in the south of the country, showed that the great majority of the 32 children in the fifth grade of the local school were already working, and that they had begun to do so at 5, 6 or 7 years of age (see below).

SECTORS OF ACTIVITY

Above all, children work in family undertakings, whether these be agricultural, commercial, service or industrial. A great many family industrial undertakings carry out home work for third parties.

Here it should be clearly stated that when children are working in family undertakings the law is not being broken.

Children also work as wage earners in small industries, in handicrafts workshops and in the services sector, especially commerce. Lastly, a small number of children are self-employed workers, principally street traders selling various articles.

Many children are engaged on a wide range of agricultural jobs and in looking after livestock, working either with their family or for an employer. They also pack, load, unload and deliver goods ; they are taken on as cleaners in bakeries and barbers' shops ; they work in hotels, bars and restaurants as waiters, shoeblacks and dish-washers ; they may be found behind the counter in a wide range of shops, selling all kinds of articles ; they are employed in small mechanical and panel-beating workshops ; they repair tyres and sell petrol ; they are engaged on making shirts, gloves, shoes and other leather goods ; they are unskilled labourers in the building industry, and so on. As regards domestic service, few Italian girls now work in this sector, having been replaced by girls of other nationalities.

A certain number of children of both sexes do jobs that are sordid in themselves or are closely related to sordid activities.

WORKING CONDITIONS AND ENVIRONMENT

For obvious reasons, working conditions in family undertakings are better than those in undertakings where children work as wage earners ; in contrast, the working environment is usually about the same in both types of undertaking.

The quality of the working environment commonly varies between good and mediocre in commerce and in the service industries and between mediocre and poor (and even worse in some places) in small local industries.

In agriculture, building, many kinds of industry and mechanical engineering workshops and the like, children work almost constantly in a dirty environment, breathing in dust, disagreeable smells and harmful vapours.

Perhaps the worst conditions of work are those of young shepherd boys and other children looking after animals, since they spend the whole day at the mercy of the weather, completely alone, badly fed and with conditions of hygiene that leave a good deal to be desired.

The length of the working day varies greatly, ranging from four to six hours for children who attend school in the normal way to a maximum of 10 to 12 hours, especially for children working in agriculture, looking after animals or working in bakeries, some commercial sectors and certain services. The majority of working children work five or six days a week, but some have no weekly rest day at all. Excessive periods of work often carried out at a very rapid rate (as in picking grapes, olives and other fruit, for example, and in certain small industries) can be highly exhausting.

In many of the jobs they do, children must lift loads that are too heavy for them ; weights of 20-25 kg are not uncommon.

It is customary to treat the working child in a contemptuous manner, and there is no lack of abuses of every kind and of ill-treatment.

In agriculture, small industries, engineering workshops and building in particular, large numbers of children meet with occupational accidents which, as they are sustained during illegal working activities, tend to be concealed both by parents and by employers. When the accident is a serious one, the employer usually makes some form of purely private arrangement with the parents for financial compensation.

REMUNERATION

In family undertakings the working child does not usually receive a fixed wage, since it is presumed that by his work he is making his contribution towards the family income as a whole. The money he receives for his personal expenses is generally considered not as a formal payment but as an internal family matter.

When the child is a wage earner, the exploitation to which he is subject is evident in his conditions of work, but is seen in perhaps its most acute form in the very low wages he receives. As every wage-earning child is breaking the law, he practically never receives the official minimum wage nor indeed any of the benefits foreseen in collective agreements ; he usually has no right to any social security benefits, nor is he insured against any occupational risks. The employer pays him a derisory wage, which is usually several times less than the minimum adult wage, even when his output is virtually the same as that of an adult doing the same job. In other words, clandestine work by children is not paid at its true worth, and the current practice is to fob them off with a small payment which is little more than a tip.

DURATION OF EMPLOYMENT

Agricultural work is mainly seasonal. At sowing and harvest times virtually everyone is out in the fields. At these times children usually do not go to school so that they can devote themselves entirely to the work in hand.

During the summer holidays too, many children find themselves a job, especially in the tourist and related industries, since in Italy the school holidays and the high tourist season coincide.

Some children do occasional work, for example when they manage to get themselves taken on as unskilled labourers on some building site.

In reality, most children who work do so throughout the year or for the greater part of it, either outside school hours or full time (because they have dropped out of school, or else because they have reached the age of 14 years and have thus completed the period of compulsory schooling). It should be made clear here that in Italy youngsters have the right to work from the age of 15 years but they end their compulsory schooling at 14 ; the fact that there is thus a gap of a year between leaving school and legally beginning work gives rise to many problems.

EDUCATION AND VOCATIONAL TRAINING

Throughout Italy, attendance at school is compulsory and free for eight years from the ages of 6 to 14 ; the first five years are spent in the primary school and the other three in the so-called "middle school". During the past few decades, the Government has made remarkable efforts in the field of education. The Italian school provides general cultural knowledge but in the middle school there are also compulsory technical education courses which prepare pupils for the vocational training courses they will be able to follow later on.

Unfortunately, there is a shortage of school buildings, and therefore, to make the best use of those that do exist, one group of pupils may attend school in the morning and another in the afternoon. This is the general rule, although some "full-time" schools are to be found.

The most serious problem of the national educational system is, however, that of school drop-outs. As they grow older, more and more children stop going to school : some may do so temporarily, others are registered as being at school but never attend, others again give up school once and for all. The basic reason is the children's entry into the labour market. For the very reason that many pupils appear on the school register, even though they do not turn up for lessons, it is very difficult to determine exactly how many children do in fact drop out of school. However, it is known that more children do so in the south and in rural areas than elsewhere.

A recent study of a representative sample of country children revealed that 52.6 per cent of children had worked to help their families at some time during the years of compulsory schooling ; 24.7 per cent had worked for third parties ; and 22.7 per cent had never worked. [5] The same study lists the various reasons given for dropping out of school and the percentages for each cause, as follows :

Reason	Percentage
Little desire to study	34.40
Prefer to work	18.85
Slow progress at school	16.90
Illness	13.00
Difficult family situation	5.85
Poor relationship with teachers	5.85
Others	8.45

In most cases two or more of these reasons act in combination. [6]

The relationship between work and attendance at school was well brought out in a table prepared by the Labour Inspectorate from data on 8,630 children caught working illegally in 1970-71, part of which is reproduced overleaf as table 12.

Many working children are able to follow school courses at the same time, without their having to leave school, especially if they work only during the school holidays and/or at certain times of the year.

There is a widespread belief that vocational training at the workplace is more effective than that given in specialised academic institutions. However, without examining the accuracy of this belief, we may observe that those children who begin work at an early age can only learn to do simple and unskilled tasks at the workplace.

LEGISLATION

The protection of children and young persons is governed by Act No. 977 of 17 October 1967. Under this Act the minimum age for admission to employment (including apprentices) is 15 years. The employment of children in agriculture, in light non-industrial work or in domestic work inherent in family life is authorised as from the fourteenth birthday, on condition that such work does not affect their health or interfere with their attendance at school.

Act No. 977 is very detailed and comprehensive, and contains clauses relating to preventive and periodic medical examinations, to the carrying and lifting of weights, to night work, to hours of work, to work breaks, weekly rest and annual vacational leave, to the social insurance coverage of illegally employed children and to children's vocational training.

Table 12. Italy : children found working illegally : attendance at school
(Percentages)

Age-group	Working children who attended school in 1970-71	Working children who had never attended school
Up to 9 years	61.3	5.9
10-11	47.6	2.7
11-12	44.6	1.3
12-13	30.0	1.7
13-14	16.9	1.0
14-15	15.5	0.4
Average	21.0	0.9

Source. Ministry of Labour and Social Welfare : *Relazione annuale sull'attività dell'Ispettorato del Lavoro 1971* (Rome, 1972), p. 87.

Decree No. 36 of 4 January 1971 gives specific details of the light non-industrial jobs that young persons who have reached their fourteenth birthday may undertake : for example, certain administrative jobs, certain jobs in the retail trade, and minor jobs in hotels and barbers' shops.

LABOUR INSPECTION

In view of the enormous number of infringements of Act No. 977, it may be said that the effectiveness of the Labour Inspectorate is limited. This is because practically no children work in the modern industrial and services sectors and because the Labour Inspectorate is not in a position to visit the countless small industrial and handicrafts workshops, clandestine or otherwise, where child labour is common. Nor is it possible for the inspectors to visit the innumerable small farms on which children are employed.

The Ministry of Labour and Social Welfare is well aware of the difficulties of enforcing Act No. 977 and accordingly organised in 1971 an inspection campaign, the sole aim of which was to detect infringements of the minimum age legislation. [7] During that campaign the inspectors visited 67,450 industrial, commercial, handicrafts and service undertakings, in which they found 8,630 young people working illegally, above all in engineering workshops, small businesses and the hotel trade. This figure may be considered to be a representative sample of the true extent of child labour in Italy as a whole. According to most subsequent estimates the figure has increased since then. In its search for practical and realistic solutions to the phenomenon of child labour in Italy, the Ministry passed the results of these inspections to the provincial trade union organisations, which recognised that a stop could not be put to child labour by repressive measures alone ; a wide range of social measures was also called for, such as the restructuring of the school system and the creation of social assistance centres.

"I DON'T PLAY, I WORK"

A recently published study with the above title aroused considerable interest throughout Italy. [8] An investigation was carried out among the fifth-year pupils in a primary school in Altamura, in the south of the country, and its findings may be considered to convey accurately the hard life of very many Italian children of school age. The main results of the investigation were as follows : of the 32 pupils in the class, 18 worked during the whole year ; they were employed on nine different jobs, most of which were in shops, in bakeries or on farms ; most of the children worked five or six hours a day, but the four bakers in the class worked 9 to 12 hours a day. As well as the 18 children who worked all day, nine worked only in the summer, in bars or in farms, with their parents ; the other five did not work. Of the 27 who did work, 17 did so for people outside the family circle (to earn more money) ; virtually none of them had any contract, because they were working illegally. Most of them worked five or six days a week, although four worked on all seven days. Most of them had no time to play, and most of them had had some form of accident at work.

Notes

[1] Ministry of Labour and Social Welfare : *Relazione annuale sull'attività dell'Ispettorato del Lavoro 1971* (Rome, 1972), p. 90.

[2] Fondazione Censis : *L'occupazione occulta* (Rome, 1976), p. 37.

[3] Armando Cocco : "Lavoro minorile apprendistato scuola", in *Formazione Domani*, Jan. 1975, p. 51.

[4] M. Luisa Piccione : "La piaga del lavoro minorile", in *Formazione Domani*, Nov.-Dec. 1974, p. 47.

[5] "Alcune considerazioni scaturite dalla riflessione a posteriori sul metodo attuato", in *Formazione Domani*, Sep. 1974, p. 36.

[6] ibid., p. 37.

[7] Ministry of Labour and Social Welfare, op. cit., pp. 72-91.

[8] *Io non gioco : lavoro !* (Altamura, ARSA, 1977).

MEXICO

Graciela Bensusan *

13

SOCIOCULTURAL BACKGROUND

The heterogeneous nature of the population which is such an outstanding feature of Mexican society is a consequence of the intense movement of migrants from the countryside to the towns, which has changed both the appearance of the country's urban areas and their social and cultural composition. To take but one example, Mexico City has not grown to its present size for purely natural reasons (the so-called natural growth rate) but largely for a social reason—that is, the phenomenon of migration.

Internal migration is linked with poverty. Generally speaking, the migrant (particularly during the past few years) has left his place of origin because of the precarious economic situation there. He goes to look for a job in the town, believing that this will be better than the job he was doing at home in the country. Moreover, he goes to the town accompanied by his wife and family. This is an important point, because it means that the sociocultural environment of working children tends to resemble that of rural families.

In general, migrants tend to cling to the traditions and customs of their place of origin. Migrants from the same town or village are often found grouped together in specific areas. Furthermore, because of their low level of schooling the decisions they take are frequently far from rational. It is highly probable that their children will adopt a more modern and more rational way of life, even though they too may live in shanty towns and under marginal living conditions. This new outlook may well stem from closer contact with urban values.

The important point here is that basically it is immaterial whether the values of the young people are modern or traditional. The real problem is that of survival, and it is essential to solve this problem.

The population of working age is constantly increasing in Mexico. Job opportunities, on the other hand, are decreasing. Such, in very general terms, is the reason behind the growth of unemployment and underemployment in

* Assistant lecturer, Department of Law, Universidad Autónoma Metropolitana, Mexico City.

the country. In a situation like this the child's earnings, like those of the mother, make an important contribution to the family income. And it is common to find that child workers come not only from the very low social classes but also from those a little higher up the social scale.

In the face of the grinding poverty in which the families of child workers live, close ties of solidarity are formed with other families in the same situation. Sometimes these ties are one of the most characteristic features of family life in these conditions. The need to survive creates a broad network of social relationships (known in Mexico as *cuatismo*) which serves as a kind of social security system (and these families have no access whatever to any form of official social security system).

The author of a recent study remarks that the people who live in shanty towns are, as it were, the scavengers of the industrial system. [1] They wear old clothes ; they carry water in tin cans ; they cover the roofs of their dwellings with left-over building materials and rejects. One day they are gardeners, the next bricklayers or drivers' mates. If they fall ill their wives go out to sell *tortillas* and prickly pears or else to wash and iron other people's clothes. The children go out to sell chewing gum or beg for food on the street.

The numbers of city dwellers living precariously in this way are steadily swollen by migrants coming to the towns from rural areas. Most of these migrants go to Mexico City, Guadalajara or Monterrey, seeking a better social and economic life than is available to them at home, where the difficulties of survival, the high rate of population growth and the increase in rural unemployment and underemployment are a permanent burden. But the number of jobs available is hardly enough to absorb this newly arrived labour force. Faced with the situation that meets them in the already overcrowded cities, the only course open to them, other than doing nothing at all, is either to carry out low-productivity jobs that do not call for any specialised knowledge or to set up on their own as shoeblacks, car washers, street traders, and so on. Of course, they have no access to any form of social security benefit.

In Mexico girls and boys traditionally carry out different jobs. From a very early age (6 or 7 years) girls learn to cook, to care for babies, to look after and clean the house, to wash, darn and iron clothes, to sew and embroider, and so forth. The boys, for their part, get up at dawn to work in the fields with their fathers before going to school. Amongst other things, they learn how to grow sugar cane, rice, maize and other crops ; how to use and look after tools, such as the *machete* and the scythe, and how to care for animals. [2]

For many years, even though the official educational policy was to make no distinction between girls and boys and even though the curriculum was the same for both sexes, there was a *de facto* distinction in that single-sex schools were widespread. This was obviously a factor influencing the future distribution of roles between men and women. The spread of mixed schools

Table 13. Mexico : child population and total population, 1970

Age		Total	Male	Female
Up to 1		1 668 633	833 502	835 131
1		1 448 508	768 184	712 324
2		1 652 995	838 599	814 396
3		1 681 537	851 468	830 069
4		1 683 837	859 764	824 073
	Up to 4	8 167 510	4 151 517	4 015 993
5		1 687 290	864 244	823 046
6		1 609 631	820 898	788 783
7		1 529 414	781 382	748 032
8		1 525 995	773 401	752 594
9		1 370 666	694 854	675 812
	5-9	7 722 996	3 934 729	3 788 267
10		1 442 429	741 138	701 291
11		1 195 000	612 640	582 360
12		1 365 149	711 060	654 089
13		1 198 775	609 989	588 786
14		1 194 821	596 288	598 533
	10-14	6 396 174	3 271 115	3 125 059
Total population		48 225 238	24 065 614	24 159 624

Source. National population census, 1970.

has put an end to this situation. Nevertheless, although there is now equality of educational opportunity for both sexes, there is a greater demand for education for male children.

As we saw above, sociocultural patterns have an influence on the type of job done by boys and girls from an early age. Within the more traditional families the woman is induced to acquire the knowledge she will need to carry out household tasks, whilst the more progressive families believe that the girls should have a "short career" in work that is appropriate for a woman. Thus the chances a woman has of undertaking productive activities are restricted, and the principle that "a woman's place is in the home" is re-affirmed. Domestic service, in which women may spend their whole life from the age of 10 onwards, is a good example of this.

SOME DATA ON POPULATION

Table 13 gives a detailed breakdown of the child population in Mexico in 1970. It will be seen that some 50 per cent of the population were less than 14 years old, and that 24.5 per cent were in the 6 to 14 age-group.

The growth rate for 1970 was one of the highest in the world (3.4 per cent) ; the hope is that it will have fallen to 2.3 per cent by the year 2000.

AGE OF WORKING CHILDREN

Despite the fact that under Mexican law young people below the age of 14 years are forbidden to work, the real situation is very different. The conditions of extreme poverty in which many children live make it necessary for them to carry out various kinds of job, from about the age of 5 or 6, in order to survive.

However, the true breadth of the problem is not known at present, since for various reasons it has not yet been possible to investigate it in sufficient detail. Moreover, whenever attempts have been made to obtain data which might cast some light on the problem, the general awareness that constitutional norms are not being observed has made it far from easy to ascertain the truth of the situation.

Census data are not, in general, fully reliable. They are even less so as regards work done by young people. However, according to the 1960 census economically active children in the 8 to 14 age-group accounted for 3.1 per cent of the total economically active population. In all, 357,800 youngsters were at work, of whom 78,719 were less than 12 years old. Working children made up 5.6 per cent of the 8 to 14 age-group (6,302,301) and 2.3 per cent of the total child population up to 14 years (15,452,107). [3]

The 1970 census found that economically active children in the 12 to 14 age-group accounted for 3.3 per cent of the total economically active population (12,909,540). The proportion for the corresponding age-group in 1960 was 2.4 per cent. A trend towards an increase in the proportion of children in the labour force has thus emerged. Furthermore, the proportion of economically active children in the 12 to 14 age-group was 11.6 per cent (3,785,745), representing 1.95 per cent of the total child population up to 14 years of age (22,286,670). [4]

Data for 1973 calculated by the General Labour Directorate for the Department of the Federal District show that, of the rather more than 1 million children between the ages of 5 and 16 living in the Federal District, 133,930 were working in fixed locations and 66,965 were working on the public highway, giving a total of 200,895 child workers. This is equivalent to 20 per cent of the total child population in that age-group.

Unofficial statistics indicate that in 1973 half a million child workers less than 14 years old were beyond the reach of legal protection. It was estimated that this figure would be 30 per cent higher in 1980. Furthermore, 1.4 million young people of 16 years of age were at work throughout the country. At that time it was calculated that 43,050 children less than 14 years old were working in the Federal District.

Another study estimated that more than 100,000 children between the ages of 7 and 14 were roaming the streets of Mexico City. Elsewhere it is stated that in 1973 104,292 children between the ages of 8 and 11 and 372,181 children between the ages of 12 and 14 were at work. These figures were expected to increase to 126,193 and 450,338 respectively by 1980. It was also estimated that 1,452,000 young people of less than 16 years of age were at work.

More recently, in 1977, a magazine article declared that an inquiry carried out on behalf of the Confederation of Workers of Mexico (specifically on behalf of the Labour Federation of Young People's Organisations) put the number of 14-year-old children exploited in the country at 1.5 million, with 200,000 of them wandering about in search of the wherewithal to survive.

Figures for 1978 given by the Office for the Defence of Young People and Families show that today 1,680,000 children less than 16 years old are at work, of whom 571,764 are less than 14 years old. Of these, 69,100 work in the Federal District.

These figures do not include those children who roam the streets on their own account, selling chewing gum, washing car windscreens, cleaning shoes, and so on, and of whom there are more than 1.5 million in Mexico.

Both the census and the unofficial figures therefore show that there is a definite trend towards an increase in the number of children less than 14 years old in the Mexican labour force.

SECTORS OF ACTIVITY

Agricultural sector

Child workers in Mexico are found to some extent in all sectors of economic activity. However, it is in the agricultural sector that child labour is the most widespread.

From about the age of 6 years onwards the child begins to carry out light tasks on the family plot, such as collecting wool and looking after animals. Then, as he learns how to use the basic agricultural hand tools, he gradually begins to help with the sowing and the harvesting (picking cotton and tomatoes, cutting sugar cane, etc.). This work, which is done within the family, is unpaid.

Nor does the child receive payment when he works with other members of the family on another person's land. In such cases the landowner arranges with the head of the family for payment at piece-work rates. The payment is made to the head of the family himself, and there is no contact in this respect between the other members of the family and the landowner.

Industrial sector

It is uncommon for large and medium-scale industries to employ children aged less than 14 years. Among the reasons for this we may mention that there is no need for them to have recourse to child labour, in view of the high level of adult unemployment in Mexico ; furthermore, child labour is of course prohibited by law.

Children are more likely to be found working in small-scale industries. Although no over-all inquiry has been made in this regard, the partial investigations that have been carried out confirm this statement. For example, an investigation into the wall-partition manufacturing industry revealed that there was a high proportion of child workers among the labour force ; in some workshops all the workers were children. In most cases, however, the children were working as assistants to their fathers ; they were occupied on the least risky part of the production process and had no relationship with the employer, who engaged the father on a piece-work basis and did not undertake to pay the child anything.

In those workshops where most of the labour force was made up of children, there was a direct relationship between the employer and the child, since instead of helping his father the child was employed as a wage earner. The majority of these workshops operate in a clandestine fashion, in that they escape the attentions of the labour inspectorate.

Child labour in a family industry is not prohibited by the Constitution. As the term "family industry" implies, labour is provided by members of the family, and the employment of children is widespread (as for example in pottery and carpet manufacture). The child is not paid for this work.

In Mexico as elsewhere, industrial home work is a flourishing activity, particularly for women and in the textile industry. Here the relationship is between the homeworker himself and the employer ; the members of the homeworker's family, who are often merely youngsters, have no contact with the employer. This may be looked upon as a kind of family or home industry.

Services sector

In the towns child workers are most commonly found in the services and small business sectors. Operating as self-employed workers, they turn up on the streets offering to clean shoes, wash car windscreens, save places in theatre or cinema queues, collect rubbish, and so on. They may also offer similar services from a fixed location.

They may perhaps be taken on as market porters (for example, at the Merced and Jamaica markets, two of the most important in Mexico City), and in self-service stores they wrap up and transport the customers' purchases. It should be mentioned here that the owners of these stores do not consider the children to be employees, since they receive no wages, their sole income being made up of the tips given to them by the customers.

Large numbers of girls less than 14 years old are found in domestic service, but there is practically no demand at all for boys in this kind of work.

Turning to the street trades, one finds that many small-scale commercial activities are undertaken by children. Itinerant street vendors sell chewing gum, sweets, newspapers and magazines, lottery tickets, and so on. Young people are also found working in the small-scale handicrafts industries, as carpenters, potters, and so on.

WORKING CONDITIONS AND ENVIRONMENT

The labour legislation does not apply to self-employed workers and there are no standards governing their conditions of work. Self-employed children do not receive a "wage" and there is no general rule regarding the length of their working day. This will depend on the type of need that the child is attempting to satisfy (whether he is working to survive, to pay something into the family income, to obtain some extra pocket money to buy some object that is important to him, etc.) and on the productivity of his occupation. In extreme cases (pressing needs, low productivity) the working day may stretch over an unbroken period of 12 hours.

Working conditions are not much better for the child porters in the markets. There are no regulations concerning the maximum permissible weight that may be carried by a child. Child porters may be harassed by the men who supervise the use of wheelbarrows, etc., and by their elders doing the same job. Often they find that the few coppers they have earned are taken from them, on the pretext that they have damaged or misplaced the barrows, or that they did not have the necessary documents entitling them to work. The worst conditions of work for child porters were found in the Merced market.

Sometimes conditions are very slightly better for young people who work as packers and loaders in the big self-service stores. Although on many occasions they are chastised or suspended for no good reason, the working environment here is not so disagreeable as in the Merced market. Although they clearly have a direct relationship with the employers, recognition of this has consistently been denied. The children receive from the cashier or other employee the equipment they need to pack and carry the customers' purchases. Very often they are ordered by another higher-placed employee to do specific jobs for the store itself.

Even though it is frequently clear that there is an employment relationship between the employer and the children, this is not accepted by the self-service stores, on the grounds that the children's income is made up exclusively of tips given to them by the customers. Consequently, they do not enjoy the right to rest days and paid holidays.

Recently, however, the Department of the Federal District has intervened to insist on certain requirements being met as regards children's conditions of work. Amongst these may be mentioned the recognition by the stores that the services provided by the children are useful ; the obligation to accept a six-hour working day, with a one-hour break for meals ; and the obligation to treat the children well, to see that they work only for the customers, to provide seats and sanitary facilities and to supervise the weight of the goods they carry.

The owners of some stores agreed to give quarterly incentives in the form of school materials, provisions and clothes and to engage only young people of 14 years of age or more.

Unlike the child porters in the Merced market, most of whom had left school some time during the primary stage, the children in the self-service stores worked hours which enabled them to complete their primary schooling.

In other services activities in which children work—for instance, in small engineering workshops and in low-class cafés—the conditions are appalling. In such jobs the direct relationship with the employer is obvious but although this relationship is generally recognised, the fact that child labour is prohibited by law leads to the constant violation of labour standards. Thus, the employer convinces the youngster that he is doing him a favour by offering him work and that the child therefore cannot ask the employer to stick to the regulations regarding daily hours of work, holidays, minimum wages, and so on. The child is therefore employed in an unstable job on or beyond the fringe of social security.

In the wall-partition manufacturing industry, children work for 10 or 12 hours a day, both when they are engaged directly and when they help their fathers. As this is piece-rate work, they accept the situation as the older workers do. In general, it was observed that children carry out the less hazardous tasks such as preparing the mixture and pouring it into the moulds. The actual baking, however, is done by children despite the fact that the rickety nature of the ovens makes them a potential source of accidents.

Moreover, from the health point of view the working conditions of children are very bad, since the mixture with which they work is made up of refuse, *adobe* and waste materials.

Finally, in these small-scale industries not the slightest attention is paid to the standards regarding the length of the working day, rest days, holidays, overtime, and so on. Both adults and child workers are in the same situation in this respect.

In family industries too, the regulations concerning working conditions are usually not observed. However, because the work here is usually carried out in the home, the child is at least less exposed to the physical and moral dangers of work on the streets.

The situation is not very different as regards child labour in agriculture. When a child works with his family on other people's estates, he usually keeps at it for 10 or 12 hours without a break, and without overtime payment. Here too, neither the child nor his family have the right to holidays or any other benefit.

REMUNERATION

The method of remuneration of working children varies according to the kind of job they do. A street trader's earnings represent the difference between the buying and selling price of his stock-in-trade (chewing gum, sweets, etc.) —a difference which, in most cases, is very small. Services on the public highway are provided according to an agreed tariff. Thus, in the case of shoe cleaning, the Shoeblacks' Union (a body which brings together all non-wage-earning workers engaged in this activity) sets the rate for this particular job. In such cases earnings are often supplemented by tips.

Tips form the sole source of income for some children—those who look after cars parked at the roadside, those who clean windscreens, those who work in markets and self-service stores, those who deliver purchases to the customer's home, and so on.

In family undertakings, both those in industry and those in agriculture, the child receives no payment for his work. In some cases the head of the family is paid for the work of the family as a whole, including that done by the children. A similar situation arises when the child helps his father in an industrial job, either inside or outside the factory.

It is uncommon for the child to receive a wage in return for his work, even when he is working directly for an employer. Sometimes the underlying reason for this is that, if the child were to be paid a wage and have fixed hours of work, holidays, etc., this would imply recognition of an "employment relationship", which would in turn impose other obligations on the employer which he had not in fact fulfilled—not to mention that he was in fact breaking the law on the employment of young persons.

Because of the lack of reliable research and studies relating to child labour, it is not possible to ascertain how much children do earn in the various jobs they do. In the case of the porters at the Merced and Jamaica markets, it was found in 1975 that their average daily income was 31.00 and 38.75 pesos respectively (at the time US$1 was equal to 12.5 pesos). In that year the average minimum wage for Mexico City was approximately 58 pesos. It should be stressed here that the adult daily wage for the jobs in question was 86.70 pesos in the Merced market and 43.20 pesos in the Jamaica market.

Where workers are paid at piece-work rates (for example, as wage earners in the wall-partition manufacturing industry) there is no difference between the adults' and the children's rates per unit.

DURATION OF EMPLOYMENT

No over-all inquiry has been made into this subject. However, as in most cases poverty is the basic reason why children work in the first place, if a child is to satisfy his basic needs and/or to help his family he will have to try to find some source of income that will last the whole year through. This does not mean that the child does not attend school ; frequently, however, he will combine school with some kind of job, particularly when he continues to live within the family circle and when the family has other sources of income.

Both the children who work all the year round (out of school hours) and those who do so at weekends or holiday times or (especially) at busy periods

Table 14. Mexico City : duration of employment of children, Merced and Jamaica markets

Period worked	Number of children in each market	
	Merced	Jamaica
All year	369	71
July-August (school holidays)	148	29
December (school holidays)	23	4
Not stated	125	1
Total number of children interviewed	665	105

Source. Department of the Federal District, Directorate-General of Labour and Social Security, Office of Economic Studies and Labour Statistics : *Resumen de estudios sobre menores estibadores del mercado de La Merced y Jamaica* (Mexico City).

such as Christmas or Father's Day can be found working in self-service stores.

An investigation carried out in the Merced and Jamaica markets showed that most of the children employed there worked throughout the year (see table 14). The position in the wall-partition manufacturing industry was similar.

EDUCATION AND VOCATIONAL TRAINING

When children are forced by necessity to seek work at an early age, they are obviously obliged to accept simple jobs which call for no previous experience or training—selling lottery tickets, guarding cars, and so forth. These jobs are by their nature low-productivity jobs, and the income they produce does not even begin to satisfy the child's basic needs.

Moreover, the child doing this kind of job remains absolutely unqualified. Even if he cleans shoes or sells tickets for years on end, he will never be more qualified to take on a better paid job than he was when he started.

The opportunities for vocational training written into the labour legislation are open only to those who work for an employer, and only to those who are 14 years old and above. Children who are younger than this, who are engaged in various activities on their own account and who must work for 10 or 12 hours a day because of the low productivity of the jobs they do, have no real chance of acquiring any vocational qualifications which would enable them to escape from the marginal situation in which they operate.

As regards the opportunities for general education, article 3 of the Constitution lays down that education provided by the State shall, inter alia, be compulsory and free. Even so, official sources revealed in 1973 that 1.3 million children were not receiving primary education. In 1978, 1.5 million children (for the most part in rural areas) had no access to primary education.

Another source indicates that in 1970 740,310 children completed their primary schooling, representing an increase of 69 per cent over the 1964 figure. If the 1970 figure is compared with the number of children who entered primary school six years earlier, it transpires that those who completed their primary education in 1970 represented only 30.6 per cent of those who began it in 1965—because 1.7 million children dropped out of primary school somewhere along the way. [5]

At the end of the 1969-70 school year, 79 per cent of those enrolled moved up to the next class and 21 per cent remained where they were. The proportions for 1971-72 were 69.5 per cent and 30.5 per cent respectively. Moreover, according to the 1970 census, only 51.6 per cent of pupils who had stayed on until the age of 14 and had finished their primary schooling continued their education further.

According to a more recent study, the number of pupils enrolled in the sixth grade in the 1975-76 school year represented only 42.86 per cent of those enrolled in the first grade six years previously, which indicates that 57.14 per cent dropped out of primary school or had to repeat a grade at some stage between the first and the fifth years. This was particularly marked at the stage of transition from the first to the second grade since, on average, enrolment for the second grade represented only 73.4 per cent of that for the first grade in the previous year. [6]

The same study analysed the 1970-76 generation, finding that the number of school leavers (1,080,431) in the 1975-76 school year represented only 40.12 per cent of the first-grade primary enrolment in 1970-71 (2,693,141) ; thus, at least 1,612,711 pupils had dropped out or had had to repeat a class. The study gave the following figures for drop-outs alone, as a percentage of the total enrolment for the school year in question : 1970-71, 11.10 per cent ; 1971-72, 9.54 per cent ; 1972-73, 9.72 per cent ; 1973-74, 9.52 per cent ; 1974-75, 8.31 per cent ; 1975-76, 7.8 per cent.

A comparison of these percentages for 1970-76 with those for 1964-70 reveals that the proportion of drop-outs has been greatly reduced.

Despite this achievement, one of the conclusions of the study is that "the primary education system is largely able to meet the demands made on it, although it shows an alarming inability to hold on to and promote the pupils ; in other words, the possibility of access to primary education is very great, but the possibilities of staying there and succeeding are considerably less".

As regards the specific problem posed by the rural sector, several factors underlie the high drop-out rate and the low level of efficiency of the educational system : the practice, common in small rural schools, whereby one teacher is responsible for several age-groups ; the fact that rural families are scattered far and wide ; the fact that the organisation of the school is similar to that of urban schools (which implies a lack of awareness of the seasonal labour needs of the agricultural sector) ; the fact that the curriculum contains elements that are of little relevance in a rural economy ; and so on. [7] However, the same study points out that it has still not been definitely established whether rural children "do not go to school because of the limited capacity of existing schools or whether it is unnecessary to expand this capacity because the rural child is engaged on agricultural tasks".

LEGISLATION

The employment of children is covered by a number of statutory provisions in Mexico. It is necessary to distinguish between those provisions that govern wage-earning employment and those relating to self-employment.

As regards wage earners, the Constitution states that : "It shall not be lawful to use the labour of young persons under 14 years of age. Young persons of between 14 and 16 years of age shall not work more than six hours a day" and that : "It shall not be lawful to employ . . . young persons under 16 years of age on unhealthy or dangerous processes or on nightwork in industry, . . . or . . . after 10 p.m. in any establishment."

In the Federal District non-wage-earning workers must obtain a work permit, delivered by the Directorate-General of Labour and Social Security. One of the conditions to be met before a permit is granted is that the applicant should be over 14 years of age. Young persons between the ages of 14 and 16 must also produce evidence of parental authority or of the person exercising that authority.

Another condition is that the applicant should know how to read and write. If he is less than 18 years old, he must have completed primary education or produce evidence of attendance at school.

It is important to point out here that when the non-wage-earning worker does not meet one or other of the official requirements, the authorities are empowered to exempt him, subject to a socio-economic analysis of his situation. Accordingly, the Directorate-General of Labour and Social Security can authorise work by children less than 14 years old, when the child's situation requires it, and issues the appropriate permit.

LABOUR INSPECTION

The labour inspector ascertains that there are no workers aged less than 14 years in the undertakings or establishments he visits. If he finds any, he suggests that the employment relationship with the child be terminated and that the wages due up to that moment be paid. Moreover, he puts on record that the Labour Law has been infringed and notifies the competent body so that the appropriate penalties may be administered.

Again, when he comes across young people between the ages of 14 and 16 years working without the appropriate permit, he requests that they be presented to the authority (the labour inspectorate itself) in order that the legally necessary permit be issued to them. He puts on record this infringement also, whilst at the same time checking that the standards on the length of the working day, rest periods and holidays are respected. In order to issue the work permit, the labour inspector asks for proof that the period of compulsory schooling has been completed, for the presence of the father or mother of the child, and for details of the undertaking in which the 14- to 16-year-old youngster is to work. Although this last is not required under the law, the labour inspectorate asks for it in order to ascertain the kind of job, the wage, the length of the working day and other working conditions of the young worker.

The penalties imposed on employers who infringe the regulations on child labour consist of a fine equivalent to between 3 and 155 times the minimum wage applicable at the time and place where these infringements occurred, depending on the circumstances and gravity of the case.

Notwithstanding these provisions, the labour inspectorate's possibilities of keeping the situation under control are very limited, since in all cases the employers conceal the engagement of children of less than 14 years old and even of older children between the ages of 14 and 16—in the first case, because they are infringing a constitutional provision, and in the second, because of working conditions that for the most part are unsatisfactory. Furthermore, in numerous workshops that employ child labour the work is carried out in a clandestine fashion.

Finally, the work of the labour inspectorate is ineffective as regards those young persons in the many street trades.

Notes

[1] Larissa Lomnitz: *Cómo sobreviven los marginados* (Mexico City, Siglo XXI, 1975).

[2] E. Fromm and M. Maccoby: *Sociopsicoanálisis del campesino mexicano* (Mexico City, Fondo de Cultura Económica, 1974), p. 249.

[3] Directorate-General of Statistics: *Censo Nacional de Población de 1960: Resumen general*, p. 73.

[4] idem: *Noveno Censo General de Población, 1970: Resumen general abreviado*, p. 11.

[5] Pablo Latapi: "Educación: Balance de un sexenio", in *Excelsior* (Mexico City), 1973, No. 7.

[6] Office of Public Education, Directorate-General of Educational Planning: *Alternativas de desarrollo del sistema educativo nacional*, Vol. 1: *Comportamiento del sistema de educación escolar (1970-1976)* (Mexico City, Nov. 1976; mimeographed).

[7] Manuel Bravo Jiménez: "La educación primaria y media", in *El perfil de México en 1980* (Mexico City, Siglo XXI), Vol. II, p. 189.

NIGERIA

Ben E. Ukpabi *

14

SOCIOCULTURAL BACKGROUND

The position of the child in Nigeria presents a curious paradox. Whilst the Nigerian child is rated far above material wealth, whilst childless couples attract sympathy and pity, and whilst most parents make sacrifices to provide as much as they can for their children, the child is nevertheless subjected to firm discipline during his upbringing—"spare the rod and spoil the child", in the words of the old proverb—and is spared no work or pursuit which the parents think will provide physical and mental training for his future life.

The child's needs and aspirations are much influenced by this traditional attitude. Whilst the child will expect his parents to attend adequately to his needs, he will at the same time realise that the resources are limited and, in any case, that it is part of the traditional upbringing that he cannot get everything he asks for, even if it is available. Accordingly, the greatest aspiration of the average Nigerian child is to acquire the necessary education to equip him to live a useful life as an adult. This education need not be purely formal. In the farming, fishing or nomadic communities, the knowledge that is necessary to become a good farmer, fisherman or nomad could be just as useful as formal education in school, although modern school education has now come to be looked upon as the surest way to succeed in a society that is continually developing along modern lines.

SOME DATA ON POPULATION

The latest reliable data on population were those produced by the 1963 national population census (see table 15).

Estimates for 1979, projected at an annual rate of 2.5 per cent over the 1963 figures, include the following :

(a) the estimated number of children 14 years old and below is about 35 million ;

---

* Assistant Director, International Labour Affairs Division, Federal Ministry of Labour, Youth and Sports, Lagos.

Table 15. Nigeria : population by age-group and sex, 1963

Age-group	Males	Females	Total	% of total population
Up to 4	4 709 918	4 839 245	9 549 163	17.2
5-9	4 360 920	4 078 378	8 439 298	15.2
10-14	3 254 573	2 682 552	5 937 125	10.7
15-19	2 501 434	2 749 750	5 251 184	9.4
20-64	12 609 577	12 732 599	25 342 176	45.4
65 and above	675 430	475 679	1 151 109	2.1
Total	28 111 852	27 558 203	55 670 055	100.0

Source. 1963 national population census.

(b) this represents about 43 per cent of the estimated total population ;

(c) the estimated number of economically active children (6 to 15 years) is about 16 million ;

(d) this represents about 20 per cent of the estimated total population.

SECTORS OF ACTIVITY

In analysing the reasons why children work, one must identify two distinct types of child labour : the type that may be considered as a form of traditional education, and the type that is imposed by economic need. In several areas it is customary to let the child begin to appreciate the dignity of labour early in life, as an important preparation for manhood. In most of the farming, fishing and nomadic communities the child is encouraged to follow his parents to the farm, fishing grounds or ranches and is allotted a job that is in line with his age and ability. Even among trading communities the child follows his parents or a master to the market, carrying and delivering goods as necessary. In the non-farming areas and among most upper-class families, the child is required by tradition to help with domestic tasks.

The type of child labour that results from economic need is found mainly among poor families. Not many children from very poor families take advantage of formal school education, and thus they are free to take on any manual jobs within their ability—partly to pass the time and partly to help the family to eke out a living.

The use of child labour in the formal sector is on the decline. But in the semi-formal sector, such as the construction industry where contractors and subcontractors abound, it is on the increase, because of the considerable amount of construction work now going on in the country. It is also on the increase in the informal sector.

There are close links between child labour, urbanisation and modernisation. The country-dwellers who flock to the towns in search of better prospects are unprepared for urban life, and both they and their children have to work to pay for the food and shelter that they took for granted at home. Thus there is a great deal of child labour in the large urban areas of Lagos, Kano, Ibadan and Aba.

Child labour (excluding the "traditional education" type mentioned above) is widespread in the usual informal sector activities, and also in family businesses in the urban areas. Work in hotels and restaurants does not seem to attract the large numbers of children that it does in other countries. Child labour in factories, even in the form of direct assistance to adult workers with no direct relationship with the employer, is virtually non-existent.

The number of children who work in domestic service is also declining, especially among girls.

As in many traditional societies, certain occupations are reserved for men and others for women. The jobs of child workers usually follow the same pattern : girls generally sell foodstuffs rather than newspapers, and are not expected to work as shoeblacks on the streets because, as well as exposing them to moral danger, this job is traditionally identified with physical disability, although increasing economic need is attracting more able-bodied people into it. Again, girls do not carry loads in urban areas, even though more and more of them can be seen carrying sand at construction sites. In traditional communities, especially where there is little opportunity for formal education, it is considered that making a girl work hard on the farm or in petty trading, depending on the locality, is good training for marriage.

WORKING CONDITIONS AND ENVIRONMENT

As many of the child workers in Nigeria are employed in the informal sector, it is not possible to talk about regulated hours of work and regular working conditions. Much, indeed, depends on the availability of work.

The physical and moral dangers to which children are exposed in the course of their work are immense, and represent the most convincing case against regular child labour. Whether in the formal, semi-formal or informal sectors, children tend to work long hours and their health may be affected as a result. As some of the jobs that child workers do (street trading and bus conducting, for example) are carried out in crowded places, children are exposed to bodily injuries or disabilities arising from motor accidents, assault and battery, or even to infectious diseases. Physical damage may also result when a child carries out work beyond his capacity—for example, permanent damage has been caused to the joints of the neck and growth has been retarded when children have carried loads that are too heavy for them.

The moral risks are even more serious, as they tend to scar the child psychologically for life. It is generally accepted that young girls cannot engage in extensive street trading activities over long periods without being exposed to the dangers of sexual assault. Young girls, especially those from poor families, are faced with the temptation of selling themselves for money in the course of their street trading activities. The degree of moral danger involved in child labour is reflected in the fact that most of the children who find themselves in remand homes tend to come from that class of children who are exposed to the vicissitudes of urban life through working on the street.

It is perhaps in the urban areas that living conditions are the most appalling. In the slums and shanty towns of the big cities the shortage of housing means that entire families live in single rooms in neighbourhoods where sanitation is virtually non-existent and where a piped water supply is almost unheard of.

The urban child who works full time is also faced with the problem of obtaining food. Since he works for most of the day, he has little time for meals and, in any case, the food available is intended merely to fill the stomach : accordingly, there is no question of the urban child labourer having a balanced diet, and he is a ready victim of malnutrition, of which the most frequent result is the disease kwashiorkor.

REMUNERATION

In the semi-formal sector, where building contractors or subcontractors hire children to move sand, bricks, and so on, payment is on a piece-rate basis and the child could earn as much as 3 Naira per day (at the time of writing US$1 = 0.79 Naira). In rural areas the child who is taken on to work on a farm is provided with food, and receives a daily wage as well, sometimes of as much as 3 Naira. The urban child street trader probably makes about the same amount on average but at times (for instance, on other workers' pay days) his earnings may be much higher. The child who helps in the family farm or business is not formally remunerated.

EDUCATION AND VOCATIONAL TRAINING

Primary education, which has been free and universal since 1976, is to become compulsory in 1979. Vocational and technical training has been considerably developed in recent years, as witness the building of many colleges of technology, the award of technical scholarships and the conclusion of international agreements for technical and vocational training abroad for Nigerians. Children are also apprenticed to such trades as welder, motor mechanic, and so on.

School drop-outs seem to be more numerous among remote farming and nomadic communities (where the accepted idea of traditional formal education has not been greatly changed by contact with Western civilisation) and among the urban poor, most of whom have no permanent housing facilities and where conditions are not congenial to settled family life, which is a precondition of schooling.

Because of the need to supplement the family earnings, there is often a tendency among poor families to discourage the child's attendance at school, since if he goes to school he cannot be out earning money.

LEGISLATION

Legislation to prevent the exploitation of child labour has existed since colonial times. The provisions at present in force are contained in the Labour Decree of 1974. Sections 58 to 63 of this Decree include a wide range of provisions designed to discourage or regulate child labour. The basic premise of these provisions is that the outright prohibition of child labour is not intended ; it is taken for granted that some children do work (as a result of the belief, mentioned above, that child labour is a means of broadening the cultural and traditional education of the child, and of the recognition that economic need can force many children to work), and the aim is to regulate child labour in the interests of the physical and mental development of the child.

LABOUR INSPECTION

Because labour inspectors usually have ready access only to undertakings in the formal sector, where relatively few child workers are employed, the role played by the labour inspectorate in respect of regular child labour is a very small one. The fact that there have been no known cases of prosecution as regards child labour since the late 1950s confirms this statement. It should also be mentioned here that the considerable expansion in industrial and commercial activities over the past ten years has greatly overstretched the labour administration machinery in Nigeria.

PAKISTAN

Sabeeha Hafeez *

15

SOCIOCULTURAL BACKGROUND

The majority of working children in Pakistan are of working class origin, although some children from upper-middle- and upper-class families which own their own businesses are introduced to the family concern when they are very young.

Some children continue with their education even though they are working as well. It is important to note that working children are not necessarily illiterate, at least not in a large city like Karachi.

Some jobs (for instance shoe manufacturing, carpet weaving, bangle manufacturing) are specific to particular ethnic groups. However, as children identify far more strongly with the poor class than with their ethnic group, the children of friends who are equally poor but of different ethnic origin are taught these skills by those who inherited them from their forebears.

According to Islamic tradition, parents are responsible for their male children until they reach the age of puberty and for their female children until they are married. It is important to bear this in mind, in view of the current movement towards Islam in Pakistan. Girls frequently marry early, and thus they cannot go to school ; or if they are already at school, they have to leave. Boys have to work to support the family, rather than having the opportunity to study. This may explain why fewer girls in the 10 to 14 age-group go to school and why more boys in this age-group are already in the labour force.

According to the 1972 census, 49.3 per cent of boys in the 10 to 14 age-group in urban Pakistan were literate, as against 39.6 per cent of the girls ; the proportion for all males in urban Pakistan was 49.9 per cent, compared with 30.9 per cent for all females. In rural areas, where traditional attitudes are still strong, the gap between male and female literacy is wider : the 1972 census indicated that 22.6 per cent of all males were literate, as against only 4.7 per cent of females. In the 10 to 14 age-group the proportions for boys and girls were 24.8 per cent and 7.1 per cent respectively. It is encour-

---

* Assistant professor, Department of Sociology, University of Karachi.

aging that the literacy rate of 10 to 14-year-old girls is some 50 per cent higher than that of the rural female population as a whole.

Of the various legal requirements in force in Pakistan concerning child labour, we should draw attention to the Children (Pledging of Labour) Act of 1933, under which the parent or guardian of a child is prohibited from pledging the labour of the child in return for payment. Any agreement drawn up for this purpose is void, and any person making such an agreement is punished with a fine.

SECTORS OF ACTIVITY

Table 16 gives data on labour force participation in 1961. As might be expected, the 10 to 14 age-group shows the lowest over-all rate, but the much higher rate in rural areas should be noted. This is mainly because agriculture in Pakistan is generally a family matter, involving both the young and the old members of the family. The young people mostly work during the sowing and reaping seasons. Moreover, agriculture is not sufficiently mechanised to make it possible to dispense with the labour of children.

All over Pakistan, very many children still work in the hand-woven carpet industry. Weaving carpets is one of the family occupations that are transmitted from generation to generation, and in view of the very large numbers of children employed in this industry we shall examine it in some detail.

Work in the carpet industry is organised in two main ways : informal, where the weavers have set up looms in their own homes, receiving the basic material from the manufacturer and being paid by him in advance (children are easily absorbed into this type of carpet manufacture) ; and formal, where the looms (about eight, on average) are installed in the manufacturer's own factory. In this second case, an adult worker is hired for each loom, and he brings along his children, whose ages may range from 8 to 12. However, the payment is made by the employer direct to the weaver, who then divides the money with his children. Payment is normally made on a piece-rate basis, usually at a rate of 40 to 60 rupees per foot (at the time of writing US$1 = 9.9 rupees), depending on the quality of the carpet.

Why are so many children employed in the carpet industry ? When we attempt to answer this question, the following points come to mind :

(a) as carpet weaving is a family occupation, even those children who are studying also work part time at making carpets ;

(b) children, with their quick minds, can easily pick up the methods and skills of carpet manufacture ;

(c) children's small hands and nimble fingers are good at tying tight knots (carpets with tight knots are sold at a higher price, since such carpets are longer lasting) ;

Table 16. Pakistan : labour force participation rates by age-group and sex, 1961
(Percentages)

Age-group	All areas		Urban areas		Rural areas	
	Male	Female	Male	Female	Male	Female
10-14	38.34	4.73	18.32	1.25	45.49	6.04
15-19	72.33	7.60	57.51	2.44	78.09	9.42
All ages, 10 and above	48.14	9.27	43.03	4.05	49.85	10.88

Source. M. Afzal : *The population of Pakistan* (Islamabad, Pakistan Institute of Development Economics), p. 87.

(d) children work faster than adults, and so do more work in a shorter time ;

(e) the demand for carpets for export is such that the Export Promotion Bureau does not wish to discourage the employment of children in the carpet industry, especially as there is in any case a shortage of labour in the industry ; and

(f) a family with many children and a relatively low income cannot afford to send all the children to school, preferring them to work. Some orphans also work in the carpet industry.

The advantage of this system to the employer is that he deals with only a few adults. As he has no employment relationship with the children, he does not have to bother about the legal provisions regarding their employment. The advantage to the adult worker is that he is not victimised.

The carpet industry is not free from occupational risks. Wool dust is absorbed into the lungs of the workers and causes tuberculosis. Children often do not use protective masks when they are working.

The shoe industry is another industry where goods are exported and where there is a shortage of skilled workers. Adults working in this industry often take their children along so that they may receive some form of apprenticeship training. This informal on-the-job training is completed within two to four years. The children receive special instruction in the preparation of the various parts of the shoe and in the whole process of shoe manufacture. In a sense, this also is a family occupation.

It is mostly in the building industry and in quarrying that children have been exploited the most. They are in effect abducted from their homes and confined in camps. They are closely watched and are severely punished and humiliated if they try to escape.

The number of children in the textile industry, at least in Karachi, has gone down since 1969 when some active trade unions proposed that children should be paid the adult rate for the job in cases where the work they did was of adult standard. This proposal was not acceptable to the employers.

PERU

René Rodríguez Heredia *

16

SOCIOCULTURAL BACKGROUND

When we speak of the young people of Peru we are in fact speaking of nearly half the people in the country, since boys and girls less than 18 years old make up 44 per cent of the total population. Any study of the situation of the child in Peru must therefore be accurately placed within the over-all context of Peruvian society. To take the problem of child labour out of a context which is basically characterised by growing unemployment and underemployment, an ever-widening gulf between the incomes of rich and poor and a pernicious imbalance between rural and urban development would be to give a caricature of the real state of affairs.

Peru is a cultural mosaic. The way in which the various pieces are fitted together leaves a good deal to be desired, however, owing to the subordinate position occupied by many of these cultures within the framework of a national society in which the influence is exercised by those who are of Spanish descent, literate, and close to the administrative centres.

The Peruvian economy [1] is based on the extraction, processing and export of primary products, especially minerals, fish meal and sugar. Traditional methods of production exist side by side with other highly sophisticated methods ; there are, however, close links between the two.

The modern sector produces approximately two-thirds of the GNP but employs only one-third of the labour force.

The Peruvian economy is highly concentrated, in the following respects :

(a) from the geographical viewpoint : 62.7 per cent of the industrial value-added is produced in Greater Lima, where 71 per cent of the industrial labour force works and where 63 per cent of the investments of the manufacturing, building and services sectors are placed ;

(b) from the production viewpoint : of 4,419 undertakings, 204 (i.e. 5 per cent) account for 8 per cent of the total social capital and their contribu-

---

* Executive President, International Institute of Research and Action for Development (INDA), Lima.

tion to the industrial gross production value is in the order of 63 per cent, whereas they employ only 3 per cent of the economically active population in the sector.

Income distribution is strikingly unjust : 25 per cent of the population receives approximately 75 per cent of the national income and consumes between 80 and 90 per cent of manufacturing production.

The greatest inequality, however, is shown by the fact that 50 per cent of the national income goes to the richest 10 per cent of the population. The poorest 10 per cent receives 1 per cent of the national income, whilst the top 1 per cent receives 31 per cent of it. Of the two components making up national income (income from work and income from property), the latter shows the greater concentration : the top 1 per cent receives 83 per cent of the income from property and the top 10 per cent receives 90 per cent, whilst the top 1 per cent receives 10 per cent of the income from work and the top 10 per cent receives 30 per cent. [2]

The over-all unemployment rate is 5.2 per cent. Underemployment is very high, being estimated at 45 per cent.

Privileged, urban and rural children

If we are fully to understand the phenomenon of child labour, the various economic and cultural customs and habits found in the different regions of Peru must be taken into account. Here we adopt the classification of children devised by Castillo Ríos. [3]

The privileged child

To those in the poorer classes, the middle- and upper-class child seems —thanks to the family's income—to collect advantages and privileges from the day he is born. The fact that he does enjoy the benefits that stem therefrom is, however, tempered by his being at the same time the victim of the distortions that these material advantages generate.

The privileged child weighs, on average, 4 kg more than poor and rural children, and is 8 cm taller. His average IQ has been put at 100.2, as against 88.21 for the children of poorer families.

Paid work is unimaginable in this group, as is unpaid family work. Furthermore, the privileged child expects other children to do domestic jobs for him that he could very well do himself. The presence of an army of servants also directly influences his attitude to work, in that from his babyhood he is used to making use of others to satisfy his wishes and needs.

The poor urban child

The most important of the factors affecting child labour in an urban environment is that of the rural-urban migration that has been a feature of Peruvian life since the 1950s.

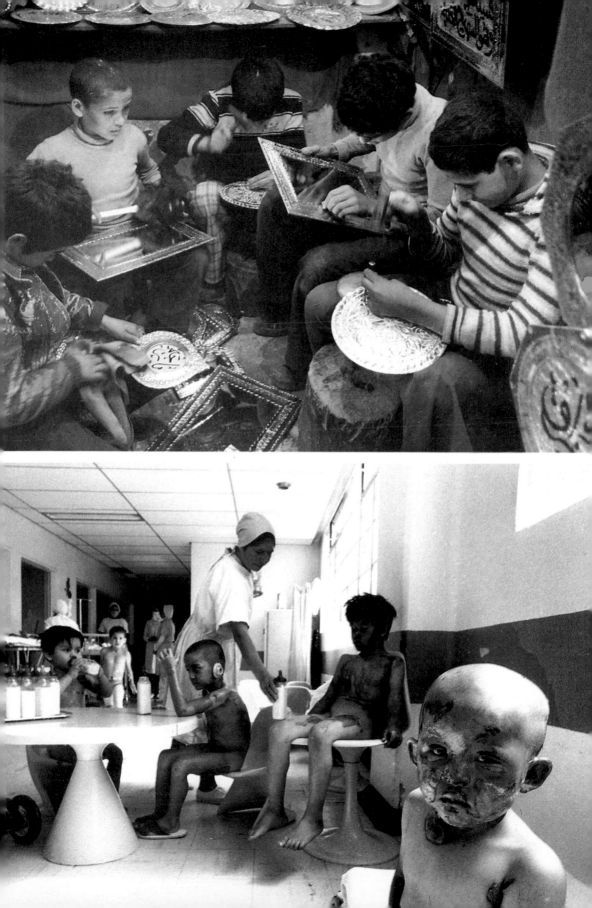

The rapid pace of urbanisation during the past 20 years and the breadth of its kaleidoscopic expansion and change have profoundly modified the Peruvian population pattern : from a country of predominantly rural settlement, it has become a predominantly urban nation. According to the National Planning Institute, the relative size of the urban population rose from 35 per cent in 1940 to 62 per cent in 1972 ; and 57.3 per cent of the urban population lives in Greater Lima.

Thus we are witnessing a "process of proletarisation. ... The massive proletarisation of Peruvian society since the 1940s is not merely a matter of the actual and formal subordination and conversion of the labour force to wage-earning employment ; it also stems from the migration, urbanisation and 'metropolitisation' of the labour force and from its transfer to the services sector or 'tertiarisation'. 'Metropolitisation' and 'tertiarisation' are two linked phenomena, in that a large number of those newly arrived in the main cities find their way into the non-industrial services sector." [4]

Pauperisation is an inseparable part of proletarisation in Peru. In the big cities it is clearly visible and statistically undeniable. It had been calculated that over 45 per cent of the national population live in shanty towns or in slums. Of these, over 60 per cent are less than 18 years old.

An investigation [5] into the educational and psychological problems of children in shanty towns led to the following conclusions, amongst others :

(a) children in the shanty towns have an average IQ of 82 ;

(b) they exhibit serious deficiencies in their ability to pay attention, in their powers of concentration, in the amount of information they can absorb and in their vocabulary ; and

(c) they exhibit serious deficiencies in visual and motor skills, which suggests biological immaturity.

From about the age of 6 or 7, which specialists call the second childhood, the child begins to realise that if his home is a cramped, gloomy place where arguments frequently break out, the street offers a vista of wide open spaces where he can lead a new life. The city seems to offer a solution to all his problems. In the street, the poor child shakes off the last unhappy memories of his indigenous origin, soaks up new ideologies, learns to live, to become a man before his time.

To quote Castillo Ríos again, "the new city dweller, getting into mischief, selling newspapers or lottery tickets, cleaning shoes, looking after and washing cars, peddling his wares or begging, begins to dominate his surroundings ; for him, the city is a stage on which he can star in a new role, an uncommon mixture of paid work, hunger, joyfulness, fear and vagrancy. On the street, the humble little Indian boy will become the shrewd and alert *cholito* or civilised Indian". [6]

In the city, the level of schooling is high (85 per cent) during the first five years of primary education ; however, as the Ministry of Education states in its report for 1972, only 82 per cent reach the end of the fifth primary grade, and only 15 per cent the fifth secondary grade (at the age of 16-17 years). Furthermore, in Peru the "alternative timetable" system operates, in which three separate timetables are available : morning, afternoon and evening (this last in the People's Colleges only).

Some 90 per cent of those registered for the morning and afternoon courses are less than 18 years old. The existence of this system of alternative timetables makes easier the possibility of the child's going out to work. The same source shows that 113,524 young people between the ages of 12 and 18 years—16.7 per cent of the total—were working in 1977. [7]

City children begin their working life virtually as soon as they can get away from the home, from about the age of 7. They enter the world of work by various routes : as errand boys, as domestic servants, as street traders. Through work, the children begin to manage by themselves and gain their independence ; they learn to get up early, to look after themselves, to finish the work that they begin (so that they can earn their living). The poor child finds his way about the streets, and at night he returns to his home exhausted, keeping what is left of his money for his mother and his brothers and sisters. He can be seen in the markets, in cinema entrances, at bus and railway terminuses, in car parks and in the main squares. In the Parada market in Lima the activities of child street traders can be seen in full swing.

This premature contact by children with the realities of life on the streets, which seems to them to be an exciting mixture of school, vagrancy and a means of livelihood, proves dangerous for young girls, since sooner or later, and always through the actions of adults, it takes on overtones of clandestine and precocious promiscuity and prostitution.

The country child

As everybody is well aware, people who live in rural areas are at the bottom of the pyramid. They constitute the most oppressed section of society and participate very little, or not at all, in any decisions that may be taken, and represent the most serious problem facing the country as a whole.

The country dwellers of Peru, who originally lived in the forests and in the mountains of the Andes, do not blindly obey the rules of the social division of labour. Men, women and children all take part in productive work and do not fall victim to the process of alienation which weighs ever more heavily on city dwellers.

The country child lives and works in a family whose activities are generally limited to meagre agricultural production. At the early age of 6, he begins to share in production work and simultaneously is introduced to the social division of labour by sex. The boys look after the sheep, gather wool, collect fodder, draw water, sow and reap. The girls milk, cook, spin, look after the other children. The country child is invariably a working child, and work is a fundamental part of his existence.

Table 17. Peru : population aged up to 19 years, by area of residence, 1961 and 1972

Year	Population aged up to 19 years	Urban	%	Rural	%
1961	5 263 800	2 440 052	46.4	2 823 748	53.6
1972	7 350 576	4 295 798	58.4	3 054 778	41.6

Source. 1961 and 1972 national population censuses.

The young handicrafts workers must not be overlooked. According to very approximate data provided by the Ministry of Industry and Tourism, there were more than half a million handicrafts workers in Peru in 1976, almost all of them living in the country or in small country hamlets. Handicrafts work in Peru is an economic activity which traditionally is handed down from father to son. It is stated that "all the boys in handicrafts families work as apprentices to their fathers". [8]

SOME DATA ON POPULATION

More than half the population of Peru is less than 19 years old (9 million out of a total of 17 million souls). A comparison of the 1961 and 1972 national population censuses reveals that the proportion of children in the towns increased from less than 50 per cent to almost 60 per cent during the 11 years between the two censuses (see table 17). Six out of every ten inhabitants of Peruvian cities live in shanty towns. The child mortality rate is 69 per cent, the main causes of death being infectious and respiratory diseases.

AGE OF WORKING CHILDREN

According to official statistics, 480,828 young people between the ages of 6 and 19 were at work in Peru in 1961, i.e. 14.6 per cent of the total number in that age-group (3,282,606). This figure represents 15.4 per cent of the total economically active population (3,124,579). The same statistics show that most of the young people concerned are in the 15 to 19 age-group. In 1972 80,710 children between the ages of 6 and 14 were at work, i.e. 2.4 per cent of the total number in that age-group (3,330,612) and 2.2 per cent of the total economically active population (3,653,036) (see table 18).

These figures should be approached with a certain amount of caution, since other bodies provide contradictory statistics : whereas the National Statistics Institute maintains that in the whole of Peru some 80,000 children of 6 to 14 years of age are employed, the Ministry of Education states that 114,000 young people are working in Greater Lima alone.

Table 18. Peru : economically active young people by age-group, 1961 and 1972

Age-group	Number of persons	Economically active population	
		Number	% of total
1961			
6-9	1 156 695	6 775	0.5
10-14	1 152 195	72 840	6.3
15-19	973 716	401 213	41.2
Total 6-19	3 282 606	480 828	14.6
Total economically active population	*7 925 482*	*3 124 579*	
1972			
6-14	3 330 612	80 710	2.4
Total economically active population	*10 909 556*	*3 653 036*	

Source. 1961 and 1972 national population censuses.
Note. In the 1972 census the economically active population was broken down into the age-groups 6-14, 15-29, etc. More detailed comparisons are therefore not possible.

SECTORS OF ACTIVITY

Modern manufacturing sector

Practically no young people are employed in this sector ; however, it is known that some undertakings do engage children for certain jobs requiring skills that can only be done by small hands (embroidery, for instance).

Small manufacturing (non-handicrafts) industry

Here child labour is more prevalent, especially for carrying spare parts and cleaning.

Ambulatory commercial sector

It is in this sector that most working children are found. By the term "ambulatory commercial sector" we do not mean the street trades, with their numerous vendors of trinkets, lottery tickets and newspapers, but the intricate system organised by the main distribution companies.

With an economically active population of which 50 per cent are employed, 45 per cent underemployed and 5 per cent unemployed, it can easily be deduced that a vast army exists to carry out ambulatory selling jobs. In Greater Lima alone, more than 300,000 people were occupied in this way in 1976.

The minimum basic wage in Greater Lima is the equivalent of US$130 a month. And if this is the official rate, it is easy to imagine what the non-official wage will be. The writer of this chapter, in a limited inquiry carried out in October 1978, found that the average daily wage was 150 soles, by way of commission. This implies a total monthly wage of 3,750 soles (= US$20) for 25 days of work and with no social security whatsoever.

This point could be examined in much greater depth, but lack of space prevents more than a passing mention.

Domestic service

The number of persons in domestic service was 175,196, according to the 1961 national population census. These people often live and work in precarious conditions.

Women make up 82 per cent of domestic servants, and 55 per cent are young people ; 12 per cent are boys or girls between the ages of 7 and 15. The 1961 census states that 17,190 children were working as domestic servants, and it is very probable that this figure has increased since then.

The Employment and Human Resources Department of the Ministry of Labour says that 37.3 per cent of all women domestic servants are girls between 14 and 19 years old. The 14 to 25 year age-group includes 74,921 women domestic servants, representing 67 per cent of the total.

Domestic servants are therefore mainly young women. They are also usually migrants : 88 per cent of them have come from all parts of the country to the big cities and to Lima itself.

Domestic servants do not take the steps that are necessary if they are to exercise their rights—only some 150-200 are members of the trade union that represents them. There are no information campaigns explaining the legislation in force on the procedure for legally defending themselves against the abuses committed by their employers.

Informal sector

As in other large Third World towns, there is a sizeable informal sector in Peruvian cities. All the jobs in this sector—shoeblacks, car washers, street singers, and so on and so forth—are done by children, who are, however, carefully organised in specific streets or districts by the adults who exploit them. These are not the self-employed shoeblacks or newspaper boys of former times. Here we are talking about informal businesses run by adults with the aim of exploiting children.

Agricultural and handicrafts sectors

These sectors have already been discussed above in the subsection "The country child".

Table 19 gives the figures for the employment of young people in Peru in 1961 and 1972.

Table 19.   Peru : employment of young people by economic sector, 1961 and 1972

Sector of economic activity	1961					1972	
	6-9 years	10-14 years	15-19 years	6-19 years	% of total	6-14 years	% of total
Agriculture, hunting and forestry	3 412	33 951	192 498	229 861	47.8	45 691	56.6
Fishing	—	—	—	—	—	298	0.3
Mining	10	194	4 474	4 678	0.9	215	0.2
Manufacturing	—	2 719	47 151	49 870	10.3	3 969	4.9
Electricity, gas and water	—	47	448	495	0.01	25	0.03
Construction	14	438	8 896	9 348	1.9	730	0.9
Commerce	89	2 134	25 200	27 423	5.7	3 962	4.9
Business services	3 160	30 276	85 898	119 334	24.8	139	0.1
Community services						21 731	26.9
Transport	3	201	4 940	5 144	1.0	765	0.9
Activities not adequately described	87	999	31 892	32 978	6.8	3 199	3.9
Total	6 775	72 840	401 213	480 828	100.00	80 710	100.00

Source. 1961 and 1972 national population censuses.

WORKING CONDITIONS AND ENVIRONMENT

Between the working country child and the humble inhabitant of the city slums and shanty towns there is a common bond : the process of migration. Basically, both are country children, with the same origins and traditions. The only real difference is that one has remained in the country and the other has moved to the city in search of new opportunities.

The country dweller who leaves his land behind him is not a happy person ; but then, neither is his brother who stays behind to "live on his poverty". In both cases, for the great majority, the conditions of life are below what is humanly desirable.

According to the Housing Development Plan for 1977-78, 63 per cent of existing dwelling-places have at the most two rooms ; five or more people are living in 65 per cent of them ; 77 per cent are made of *adobe* (sun-dried brick), *quincha* (reed-bound walls), matting, mud and similar materials ; in the shanty towns and slums where half the population of Peru lives, the average area for 7.11 persons is 12.83 square metres.

It is not difficult to deduce what the consequences of living in such an environment must be : promiscuity, skin diseases, and so on. As Castillo Ríos says, "owing to the lack of peace and quiet that is typical of over-populated homes, the child practically lives in public. People are constantly getting in each others' way, and noise and animals are everywhere ...". [9]

With regard to food, Dr. Antonio Meza Cuadra declares that "the average daily intake of calories per person in Peru is 1,900, which is nearer to the mortality level (1,400 calories) than to the minimum recommended by the Food and Agriculture Organization of the United Nations (2,500). The protein intake is more than 50 per cent below the desirable minimum." [10]

Finally, if the situation regarding occupational safety and health is very bad for adult workers, it is infinitely more so for young working people, in as much as they constitute a group of second-class workers.

EDUCATION AND VOCATIONAL TRAINING

Of the economically active population of Peru in 1972, 26.7 per cent were illiterate, 47.3 per cent had primary education only, 20.3 per cent had secondary education and only 0.4 per cent had higher education.

If we follow the progress through school of all Peruvian children who entered school at the age of 5 in 1964 we find that only 57.5 per cent of them completed primary education, only 20 per cent completed secondary education and only 2.5 per cent completed higher education (see figure 1). The figures for school drop-outs therefore give a gloomy picture of the qualifications acquired by children who leave school early to begin work. However, the official statistics show that the opportunities for technical vocational training are considerable, since 772 schools (which can take 131,087 students) specialise in basic technical education (we shall omit the SENATI and the specialised vocational skill centres, since these all cater for persons over 18 years of age).

As tables 20 and 21 show, the educational level of the economically active population as a whole is rather low. The 1961 national population census provided valuable information on the educational and employment situation of young people between the ages of 15 and 19, which is reproduced in tabular form in table 22.

LEGISLATION

The legal provisions governing the employment of children in Peru are four in number : Act No. 2851 to Regulate the Employment of Women and Children, of 25 November 1918 ; Act No. 4239 modifying the above Act ; the Supreme Decree regulating the previous Acts ; and the Young Persons Code of 1962.

These are the only legal instruments on the subject ; they are somewhat general in nature and are ill adapted to the true situation.

The term "employment of children" is interpreted as follows :

(a) it applies to work carried on in *all* kinds of occupations on behalf of an employer by young persons under 14 years of age ;

Figure 1. Peru : school drop-out levels

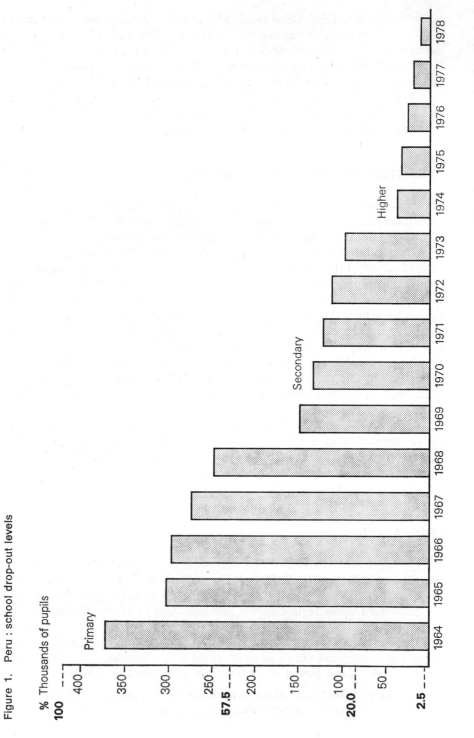

Table 20.   Peru : matriculation and drop-out levels, boys and girls aged 6-14 years, 1965 and 1970
(Thousands)

Age	Total		Matriculation		Drop-outs	
	1965	1970	1965	1970	1965	1970
Boys						
6	186.3	208.8	88.7	120.9	97.6	87.9
7	179.2	203.5	118.2	150.4	61.0	53.3
8	170.6	198.9	125.4	163.3	45.2	35.6
9	162.1	194.5	126.4	164.9	35.7	29.6
10	154.6	183.0	127.8	161.7	26.8	21.3
11	147.7	184.2	115.3	151.6	32.4	32.6
12	141.7	177.4	118.1	146.7	23.6	30.7
13	136.6	169.0	103.9	136.3	32.7	32.7
14	132.5	160.0	98.5	125.1	34.0	35.5
Total	411.3	1 679.9	1 022.3	1 320.9	389.0	350.0
Girls						
6	180.4	203.5	83.8	114.4	96.6	89.1
7	175.5	198.4	107.3	138.7	68.2	59.7
8	167.3	193.9	110.6	138.0	56.7	55.9
9	159.2	189.6	109.3	147.9	49.9	41.7
10	150.7	177.3	109.8	144.3	40.9	33.0
11	143.9	178.3	98.1	131.4	45.8	46.9
12	138.0	173.9	96.1	122.1	41.9	51.8
13	139.1	165.8	80.3	106.3	52.8	59.5
14	129.1	157.7	70.7	91.3	58.4	66.4
Total	377.2	1 638.4	866.0	1 134.4	511.2	504.0

Source. Ministry of Education : *Demanda y oferta de educación, período 1965-1972, Peru.*

(b) it does not apply to work done under the authority and supervision of parents, without the assistance of any persons not members of the family ;

(c) it does not apply to domestic service ; and

(d) it does not apply to agricultural occupations in which mechanical power is not used.

The term "minimum age for admission to employment" is interpreted as follows :

(a) 14 years for agricultural work ; 15 years for industrial work ; 16 years for work in commercial fishery ; and

Table 21. Peru : distribution of economically active population by educational level, 1961
(Percentages)

Educational level	Distribution of total economically active population	Distribution of economically active population aged 6-14
No level attained	32.8	38.2
Primary education	52.2	57.6
Grades 1 to 3	27.4	
Grades 4 to 5	24.8	
Secondary education	11.1	4.5
Grades 1 to 3	5.8	
Grades 4 to 5	5.3	
Higher education	2.3	
Not specified	—	0.2
Total	100.0	100.0

Source. 1961 national population census.

Table 22. Peru : breakdown of the 15 to 19 age-group by activity, 1961

Activity	Number of persons so engaged	
Studying only	298 735	329 263 studying
Studying and working	30 510	
Working only	370 703	401 213 working
Others	273 750	

Source. 1961 national population census.

(b) children under the age of 14 years but above 12 may be employed if :
  (i) they are able to read, write and reckon ;
  (ii) they produce a medical certificate of their physical fitness for the work in which they are to be employed.

The working hours for children less than 14 years old are not to exceed six in any one day and 33 in any one week.

The Child Employment Department of the Subdirectorate of Inspection Services is responsible for supervising the application of this legislation. In Lima this work is undertaken by two officials, in the south by one and in the north by none.

To resume :

(*a*) Peruvian legislation on the employment of children is very antiquated and out of touch with reality. Its scope is very general and in practice it is hardly ever applied ;

(*b*) Peru has ratified none of the international labour Conventions relating directly to the employment of children and young persons (Conventions Nos. 5, 6 and 138) ;

(*c*) given the very limited number of staff available, the effectiveness of the Child Employment Department leaves a good deal to be desired, with only a few conscientious employers taking any notice of it ;

(*d*) the Child Employment Department is a body which accumulates files but which provides no active protection of child workers. An important fact to be noted here is that from 1970 to the date of writing no sanctions have been applied by it ;

(*e*) the legislation does not provide that parents or guardians should act as intermediaries in dealings with the employers, leaving all negotiations to the child himself ; and

(*f*) legislation on the protection of women and children is in open contradiction with existing standards on domestic service :

   (i) domestic service is not considered to be wage-earning employment ;

   (ii) a child working in domestic service does not require a permit to do so ;

   (iii) his workplace is not subject to inspection by officials of the Ministry of Labour ;

   (iv) there are no standards on minimum salary ; and

   (v) he has the right to only 15 days holiday a year.

Notes

[1] The data on the Peruvian economy are taken from ILO : *Informe al Gobierno del Perú sobre las labores de la Misión multidisciplinaria del PIACT (3 de agosto - 8 de septiembre de 1977)* (Geneva, 1977), pp. 7-18.

[2] Adolfo Figueroa : *El impacto de las reformas actuales sobre la distribución de ingresos en el Perú (1968-1972)* (Lima, Pontificia Universidad Católica del Perú, 1973).

[3] C. Castillo Ríos : *Los niños del Perú* (Lima, Editorial Universo, 1975).

[4] Etienne Henry : *La escena urbana* (Lima, Pontificia Universidad Católica del Perú, 1978), p. 61.

[5] *Hacia una educación más humana* (Lima, Universidad de San Marcos, 1960).

[6] Castillo Ríos, op. cit., p. 140.

[7] See MARKA, 1978, No. 14, p. 26.

[8] Ministry of Industry and Tourism : *Plan Sectorial de Industrias* (Lima, 1976).

[9] Castillo Ríos, op. cit., p. 123.

[10] Antonio Meza Cuadra : *Nivel de vida y salud* (Lima, Editorial Causachum, 1972).

THAILAND

17

Benjamas Prachankhadee *
Amphorn Nelayothin
Naengnoi Intrasukporn
Vinat Montawan

SOCIOCULTURAL BACKGROUND

The typical Thai family is the extended family comprising parents, brothers, sisters, children, grandparents, and so on, in which close family ties are maintained. These families usually have little knowledge of family planning, and so are frequently too large for the adults to support on their own, so that the children have to begin work at an early age. Poor children are often neglected and their living conditions are generally bad.

SOME DATA ON POPULATION

In 1971 56.2 per cent of the population of Thailand were under 19 years old. By 1976 this proportion had fallen slightly, to 55.8 per cent.

In 1971 962,430 children between the ages of 11 and 14 years were at work, representing 5.78 per cent of the total labour force. The figures for 1976 were 985,770 and 5.31 per cent respectively.

SECTORS OF ACTIVITY

Table 23 shows the number of working children between the ages of 7 and 19 by age-group, sex and work status. It emerges very clearly from this table that by far the majority of children in rural areas are unpaid family workers. These children are mainly engaged on agricultural work.

Since the preparation of table 23, however, the number of children migrating to the towns has risen to hundreds of thousands. These boys and

---

* Acting Chief, Women and Children Section, Labour Protection Division, Department of Labour, Bangkok. Mrs. Prachankhadee led the team of research workers, who are all officials of the Department of Labour.

Table 23. Thailand : estimated child labour force by age-group, sex and work status, 1975

Work status	Boys			Girls		
	7-10	11-14	15-19	7-10	11-14	15-19
Urban areas						
Private employee	—	3 330	49 020	160	8 170	63 240
Unpaid family worker	80	2 650	21 430	90	3 760	26 460
Others	—	1 060	9 870	—	820	10 820
Total	80	7 040	80 320	250	12 750	100 520
Rural areas						
Private employee	—	21 700	164 110	—	21 690	159 450
Self-employed	—	6 620	36 450	—	6 890	54 290
Unpaid family worker	5 080	316 720	1 083 440	6 760	370 120	1 166 760
Total	5 080	348 520	1 290 000	6 760	398 700	1 384 860

Source. Office of the Prime Minister, National Statistical Office : *Children and youth survey, Thailand, 1975* (Bangkok).

girls have neither education nor experience. They come mainly from the highlands in the north-east. The industrial sectors in which children are employed include glass manufacture, food canning, garments, cold storage, ornament and toy manufacture, and so on.

Children are also employed in a wide variety of jobs in the services sector. For instance, most waiters and waitresses are between 12 and 15 years old. The work is light, but is often unbroken for long periods ; the working day varies between 9 and 11 or 12 hours, without rest or holidays. These children are mostly from outlying rural areas. They live in the restaurants and are given free meals.

One unusual trade which is open to boys is that of jockey. Boys aged between 13 and 16 years old are in great demand. They are obliged to practise horse riding every morning and every afternoon. Nevertheless, they have enough time to relax, and they also go to school and receive good pay. At weekends in particular they earn enough to support their families.

Both boys and girls are engaged in the typical street trades of flower and newspaper selling. Most of them are between 10 and 15 years old and are still at school ; they take the job as a part-time activity. Their income is high, and the work is popular in spite of its risky nature.

Boys of 12 to 15 years of age are also employed as caddies at golf courses and as ball boys at tennis courts. Their working hours are from early morning until late at night. They are paid on a monthly basis, and usually receive tips as well.

No occupation is traditionally reserved for boys or for girls. The choice is up to the employers and often depends on the ability of the children themselves. Usually boys are employed on the more hazardous jobs such as those in the metal or plastics industries. The jobs that girls do are mainly in the garments industry and in glass factories.

WORKING CONDITIONS AND ENVIRONMENT

The working conditions of children vary according to the type of job on which they are engaged. We shall therefore examine in more detail some of the industrial activities which children habitually perform.

Glass industry [1]

There are only two or three modern glass factories in Thailand ; their employees are all over 18 years old. Other glass factories are mostly small and employ children from the age of 11 years onwards. When they first begin work, they are assigned to moving sheets of glass. These smaller undertakings are generally situated in wooden houses ; the floor is of earth or cement and the rooms are generally stuffy and hot, with poor lighting (the offices of the manager and administrative staff are generally air-conditioned). Some factories may have sufficient ventilation. In these conditions it is almost inevitable that children should suffer from the heat. [2]

Work in the glass industry is carried on all round the clock. Working hours for children vary according to the size of the factory. At present, the working day generally starts at 7.30 a.m. and continues until 4.30 or 5 p.m. During the working day there are three or four breaks, each lasting 15 minutes, when children can wash their faces to gain relief from the heat. There is a one-hour lunch break, followed by an afternoon interval. However, even with these fairly frequent breaks, the working children are exposed to danger.

The weekly rest day is Sunday, but as the children are employed on a daily basis they do not receive any pay for that day. As regards annual holidays, the children usually receive five or six days, of which two or three days are taken up by the Chinese New Year.

Cold storage service

The cold storage industry, which is concerned with the preservation of seafood for export as well as of fresh food, employs a great deal of child labour. The children employed are usually between the ages of 12 and 15, and come both from rural areas and from Bangkok itself. They are paid on an hourly and monthly basis. Their main job is to sort seafood such as prawns and squids into different sizes, and to clean, pack and weigh it. Sometimes they have to steam prawns before they are packed.

The number of child workers in these factories varies between 30 and 50. The factories are large and have good lighting and ventilation systems. However, the floor is often flooded with the water used for cleaning the seafood, and the children work on their feet all the time.

Working hours depend on the amount of seafood to be sorted. On some days the children may work from 8.30 a.m. to 5.30 p.m. or later ; on other days, however, working hours are shorter, and sometimes there is no work at all. This is a problem, as the children are paid at an hourly rate. A weekly rest day is provided for, but the number of days of annual leave is lower than that stipulated by the law.

The treatment afforded to workers in the cold storage industry varies. Experienced workers are given free board and lodging, a bonus, shoes and gloves. Generally, the children are given free clothing, gloves and shoes. But in some cases the workers have to pay for these services, and do not benefit from welfare services such as board and lodging, free meals and medical facilities.

Canned food industry

This industry covers foods such as sweets, toffees, noodles, sausages, ham and so on. Most of the children employed in this industry are engaged in packing sweets and toffees. The larger factories are air-conditioned, but they are few in number. [3] Most of the factories are two- or three-storey buildings : the work is done on the ground floor whilst the living accommodation for the employers and the workers from country areas is on the first floor ; children from the country areas live on the second floor, if there is one. Both the working area and the living quarters tend to be dirty and crowded. The workers sit in rows on long benches ; the lighting and ventilation are poor ; the work is fast and unbroken, with neither rest nor relaxation for the workers. In any case, they usually work overtime to earn extra money. Payment is on a monthly or daily basis. Neither employers nor employees take much notice of official rules and regulations on conditions of work.

In theory, working hours are from 8 a.m. to 5 p.m. ; in practice, however, working hours vary according to the employees' wishes. Employees from country areas start work very early in the morning and work until 10 or 11 o'clock at night. Whether weekly or public holidays are observed depends largely on the employers. Since the employers are Chinese, they usually give holidays for the Chinese New Year.

In some factories free meals are provided, whereas in others the employers give free rice but the workers have to pay for other food.

REMUNERATION

The wages earned by children vary according to the job. Although the labour law fixes the minimum wage for children at the same rate as that for adults, child workers are in fact paid at a rate that is lower than the legal rate. Because children are mainly engaged in light and easy unskilled work and do not have the same responsibilities as adults, the employers believe that they can pay whatever wage they like. In many cases children receive barely half the adult wage ; but as they have no collective bargaining power, they never seek an increase in their wage.

DURATION OF EMPLOYMENT

Children in rural areas start work sooner than those in urban areas, usually as unpaid labour on the family plot. At the end of the harvest those children whose education is at an end move into the town, where their relatives or an employment agency find them a job on a yearly contract basis. The parents receive part of the wages in advance and the rest is paid by instalments. These yearly contracts are generally renewable.

Thus there is a trend for child workers to move from agriculture to industry, albeit small-scale industry. Some children take on seasonal employment when the harvest is in, and some employers prefer this because in such cases payment is on a daily basis. There are, too, children who leave home without their parents' consent, and their parents may come at any time to take them back. Generally speaking, therefore, children do not take permanent jobs : some wish to continue studying, others to return home, and so on.

Notes

[1] *An evaluation report on working conditions of women and child labour in glass industry* (Bangkok, Department of Labour, Women and Children Section, 1974), p. 2.

[2] Surangrat Atthasatsri : *Working condition of child labour in the glass industry in Bangkok metropolis,* thesis prepared for the Faculty of Social Administration, Thammasat University, 1974, pp. 43-50.

[3] *Report of the evaluation and survey on working conditions of women and child labour in canned food factory* (Bangkok, Department of Labour, Women and Children Section, 1976), p. 7.

APPENDICES

CONVENTION CONCERNING MINIMUM AGE FOR ADMISSION TO EMPLOYMENT *

The General Conference of the International Labour Organisation,

Having been convened at Geneva by the Governing Body of the International Labour Office, and having met in its Fifty-eighth Session on 6 June 1973, and

Having decided upon the adoption of certain proposals with regard to minimum age for admission to employment, which is the fourth item on the agenda of the session, and

Noting the terms of the Minimum Age (Industry) Convention, 1919, the Minimum Age (Sea) Convention, 1920, the Minimum Age (Agriculture) Convention, 1921, the Minimum Age (Trimmers and Stokers) Convention, 1921, the Minimum Age (Non-Industrial Employment) Convention, 1932, the Minimum Age (Sea) Convention (Revised), 1936, the Minimum Age (Industry) Convention (Revised), 1937, the Minimum Age (Non-Industrial Employment) Convention (Revised), 1937, the Minimum Age (Fishermen) Convention, 1959, and the Minimum Age (Underground Work) Convention, 1965, and

Considering that the time has come to establish a general instrument on the subject, which would gradually replace the existing ones applicable to limited economic sectors, with a view to achieving the total abolition of child labour, and

Having determined that this instrument shall take the form of an international Convention,

adopts this twenty-sixth day of June of the year one thousand nine hundred and seventy-three the following Convention, which may be cited as the Minimum Age Convention, 1973 :

Article 1

Each Member for which this Convention is in force undertakes to pursue a national policy designed to ensure the effective abolition of child labour and to raise progressively the minimum age for admission to employment or work to a level consistent with the fullest physical and mental development of young persons.

---

* Convention No. 138.

147

Article 2

1. Each Member which ratifies this Convention shall specify, in a declaration appended to its ratification, a minimum age for admission to employment or work within its territory and on means of transport registered in its territory ; subject to Articles 4 to 8 of this Convention, no one under that age shall be admitted to employment or work in any occupation.

2. Each Member which has ratified this Convention may subsequently notify the Director-General of the International Labour Office, by further declarations, that it specifies a minimum age higher than that previously specified.

3. The minimum age specified in pursuance of paragraph 1 of this Article shall not be less than the age of completion of compulsory schooling and, in any case, shall not be less than 15 years.

4. Notwithstanding the provisions of paragraph 3 of this Article, a Member whose economy and educational facilities are insufficiently developed may, after consultation with the organisations of employers and workers concerned, where such exist, initially specify a minimum age of 14 years.

5. Each Member which has specified a minimum age of 14 years in pursuance of the provisions of the preceding paragraph shall include in its reports on the application of this Convention submitted under article 22 of the Constitution of the International Labour Organisation a statement—

(a) that its reason for doing so subsists ; or

(b) that it renounces its right to avail itself of the provisions in question as from a stated date.

Article 3

1. The minimum age for admission to any type of employment or work which by its nature or the circumstances in which it is carried out is likely to jeopardise the health, safety or morals of young persons shall not be less than 18 years.

2. The types of employment or work to which paragraph 1 of this Article applies shall be determined by national laws or regulations or by the competent authority, after consultation with the organisations of employers and workers concerned, where such exist.

3. Notwithstanding the provisions of paragraph 1 of this Article, national laws or regulations or the competent authority may, after consultation with the organisations of employers and workers concerned, where such exist, authorise employment or work as from the age of 16 years on condition that the health, safety and morals of the young persons concerned are fully protected and that the young persons have received adequate specific instruction or vocational training in the relevant branch of activity.

Article 4

1. In so far as necessary, the competent authority, after consultation with the organisations of employers and workers concerned, where such exist, may exclude from the application of this Convention limited categories of employment or work in respect of which special and substantial problems of application arise.

2. Each Member which ratifies this Convention shall list in its first report on the application of the Convention submitted under article 22 of the Constitution

of the International Labour Organisation any categories which may have been excluded in pursuance of paragraph 1 of this Article, giving the reasons for such exclusion, and shall state in subsequent reports the position of its law and practice in respect of the categories excluded and the extent to which effect has been given or is proposed to be given to the Convention in respect of such categories.

3. Employment or work covered by Article 3 of this Convention shall not be excluded from the application of the Convention in pursuance of this Article.

Article 5

1. A Member whose economy and administrative facilities are insufficiently developed may, after consultation with the organisations of employers and workers concerned, where such exist, initially limit the scope of application of this Convention.

2. Each Member which avails itself of the provisions of paragraph 1 of this Article shall specify, in a declaration appended to its ratification, the branches of economic activity or types of undertakings to which it will apply the provisions of the Convention.

3. The provisions of the Convention shall be applicable as a minimum to the following : mining and quarrying ; manufacturing ; construction ; electricity, gas and water ; sanitary services ; transport, storage and communication ; and plantations and other agricultural undertakings mainly producing for commercial purposes, but excluding family and small-scale holdings producing for local consumption and not regularly employing hired workers.

4. Any Member which has limited the scope of application of this Convention in pursuance of this Article—

(a) shall indicate in its reports under article 22 of the Constitution of the International Labour Organisation the general position as regards the employment or work of young persons and children in the branches of activity which are excluded from the scope of application of this Convention and any progress which may have been made towards wider application of the provisions of the Convention ;

(b) may at any time formally extend the scope of application by a declaration addressed to the Director-General of the International Labour Office.

Article 6

This Convention does not apply to work done by children and young persons in schools for general, vocational or technical education or in other training institutions, or to work done by persons at least 14 years of age in undertakings, where such work is carried out in accordance with conditions prescribed by the competent authority, after consultation with the organisations of employers and workers concerned, where such exist, and is an integral part of—

(a) a course of education or training for which a school or training institution is primarily responsible ;

(b) a programme of training mainly or entirely in an undertaking, which programme has been approved by the competent authority ; or

(c) a programme of guidance or orientation designed to facilitate the choice of an occupation or of a line of training.

Article 7

1. National laws or regulations may permit the employment or work of persons 13 to 15 years of age on light work which is—

(a) not likely to be harmful to their health or development ; and

(b) not such as to prejudice their attendance at school, their participation in vocational orientation or training programmes approved by the competent authority or their capacity to benefit from the instruction received.

2. National laws or regulations may also permit the employment or work of persons who are at least 15 years of age but have not yet completed their compulsory schooling on work which meets the requirements set forth in subparagraphs *(a)* and *(b)* of paragraph 1 of this Article.

3. The competent authority shall determine the activities in which employment or work may be permitted under paragraphs 1 and 2 of this Article and shall prescribe the number of hours during which and the conditions in which such employment or work may be undertaken.

4. Notwithstanding the provisions of paragraphs 1 and 2 of this Article, a Member which has availed itself of the provisions of paragraph 4 of Article 2 may, for as long as it continues to do so, substitute the ages 12 and 14 for the ages 13 and 15 in paragraph 1 and the age 14 for the age 15 in paragraph 2 of this Article.

Article 8

1. After consultation with the organisations of employers and workers concerned, where such exist, the competent authority may, by permits granted in individual cases, allow exceptions to the prohibition of employment or work provided for in Article 2 of this Convention, for such purposes as participation in artistic performances.

2. Permits so granted shall limit the number of hours during which and prescribe the conditions in which employment or work is allowed.

Article 9

1. All necessary measures, including the provision of appropriate penalties, shall be taken by the competent authority to ensure the effective enforcement of the provisions of this Convention.

2. National laws or regulations or the competent authority shall define the persons responsible for compliance with the provisions giving effect to the Convention.

3. National laws or regulations or the competent authority shall prescribe the registers or other documents which shall be kept and made available by the employer ; such registers or documents shall contain the names and ages or dates of birth, duly certified wherever possible, of persons whom he employs or who work for him and who are less than 18 years of age.

Article 10

1. This Convention revises, on the terms set forth in this Article, the Minimum Age (Industry) Convention, 1919, the Minimum Age (Sea) Convention, 1920, the Minimum Age (Agriculture) Convention, 1921, the Minimum Age (Trimmers and Stokers) Convention, 1921, the Minimum Age (Non-Industrial Employment) Con-

vention, 1932, the Minimum Age (Sea) Convention (Revised), 1936, the Minimum Age (Industry) Convention (Revised), 1937, the Minimum Age (Non-Industrial Employment) Convention (Revised), 1937, the Minimum Age (Fishermen) Convention, 1959, and the Minimum Age (Underground Work) Convention, 1965.

2. The coming into force of this Convention shall not close the Minimum Age (Sea) Convention (Revised), 1936, the Minimum Age (Industry) Convention, (Revised), 1937, the Minimum Age (Non-Industrial Employment) Convention (Revised), 1937, the Minimum Age (Fishermen) Convention, 1959, or the Minimum Age (Underground Work) Convention, 1965, to further ratification.

3. The Minimum Age (Industry) Convention, 1919, the Minimum Age (Sea) Convention, 1920, the Minimum Age (Agriculture) Convention, 1921, and the Minimum Age (Trimmers and Stokers) Convention, 1921, shall be closed to further ratification when all the parties thereto have consented to such closing by ratification of this Convention or by a declaration communicated to the Director-General of the International Labour Office.

4. When the obligations of this Convention are accepted—

(a) by a Member which is a party to the Minimum Age (Industry) Convention (Revised), 1937, and a minimum age of not less than 15 years is specified in pursuance of Article 2 of this Convention, this shall *ipso jure* involve the immediate denunciation of that Convention,

(b) in respect of non-industrial employment as defined in the Minimum Age (Non-Industrial Employment) Convention, 1932, by a Member which is a party to that Convention, this shall *ipso jure* involve the immediate denunciation of that Convention,

(c) in respect of non-industrial employment as defined in the Minimum Age (Non-Industrial Employment) Convention (Revised), 1937, by a Member which is a party to that Convention, and a minimum age of not less than 15 years is specified in pursuance of Article 2 of this Convention, this shall *ipso jure* involve the immediate denunciation of that Convention,

(d) in respect of maritime employment, by a Member which is a party to the Minimum Age (Sea) Convention (Revised), 1936, and a minimum age of not less than 15 years is specified in pursuance of Article 2 of this Convention or the Member specifies that Article 3 of this Convention applies to maritime employment, this shall *ipso jure* involve the immediate denunciation of that Convention,

(e) in respect of employment in maritime fishing, by a Member which is a party to the Minimum Age (Fishermen) Convention, 1959, and a minimum age of not less than 15 years is specified in pursuance of Article 2 of this Convention or the Member specifies that Article 3 of this Convention applies to employment in maritime fishing, this shall *ipso jure* involve the immediate denunciation of that Convention,

(f) by a Member which is a party to the Minimum Age (Underground Work) Convention, 1965, and a minimum age of not less than the age specified in pursuance of that Convention is specified in pursuance of Article 2 of this Convention or the Member specifies that such an age applies to employment underground in mines in virtue of Article 3 of this Convention, this shall *ipso jure* involve the immediate denunciation of that Convention,

if and when this Convention shall have come into force.

5. Acceptance of the obligations of this Convention—

(a) shall involve the denunciation of the Minimum Age (Industry) Convention, 1919, in accordance with Article 12 thereof, *(b)* in respect of agriculture shall involve the denunciation of the Minimum Age (Agriculture) Convention, 1921, in accordance with Article 9 thereof,

(c) in respect of maritime employment shall involve the denunciation of the Minimum Age (Sea) Convention, 1920, in accordance with Article 10 thereof, and of the Minimum Age (Trimmers and Stokers) Convention, 1921, in accordance with Article 12 thereof,

if and when this Convention shall have come into force.

Article 11

The formal ratifications of this Convention shall be communicated to the Director-General of the International Labour Office for registration.

Article 12

1. This Convention shall be binding only upon those Members of the International Labour Organisation whose ratifications have been registered with the Director-General.

2. It shall come into force twelve months after the date on which the ratifications of two Members have been registered with the Director-General.

3. Thereafter, this Convention shall come into force for any Member twelve months after the date on which its ratification has been registered.

Article 13

1. A Member which has ratified this Convention may denounce it after the expiration of ten years from the date on which the Convention first comes into force, by an act communicated to the Director-General of the International Labour Office for registration. Such denunciation shall not take effect until one year after the date on which it is registered.

2. Each Member which has ratified this Convention and which does not, within the year following the expiration of the period of ten years mentioned in the preceding paragraph, exercise the right of denunciation provided for in this Article, will be bound for another period of ten years and, thereafter, may denounce this Convention at the expiration of each period of ten years under the terms provided for in this Article.

Article 14

1. The Director-General of the International Labour Office shall notify all Members of the International Labour Organisation of the registration of all ratifications and denunciations communicated to him by the Members of the Organisation.

2. When notifying the Members of the Organisation of the registration of the second ratification communicated to him, the Director-General shall draw the attention of the Members of the Organisation to the date upon which the Convention will come into force.

Article 15

The Director-General of the International Labour Office shall communicate to the Secretary-General of the United Nations for registration in accordance with

Article 102 of the Charter of the United Nations full particulars of all ratifications and acts of denunciation registered by him in accordance with the provisions of the preceding Articles.

Article 16

At such times as it may consider necessary the Governing Body of the International Labour Office shall present to the General Conference a report on the working of this Convention and shall examine the desirability of placing on the agenda of the Conference the question of its revision in whole or in part.

Article 17

1. Should the Conference adopt a new Convention revising this Convention in whole or in part, then, unless the new Convention otherwise provides—

(a) the ratification by a Member of the new revising Convention shall *ipso jure* involve the immediate denunciation of this Convention, notwithstanding the provisions of Article 13 above, if and when the new revising Convention shall have come into force ;

(b) as from the date when the new revising Convention comes into force this Convention shall cease to be open to ratification by the Members.

2. This Convention shall in any case remain in force in its actual form and content for those Members which have ratified it but have not ratified the revising Convention.

Article 18

The English and French versions of the text of this Convention are equally authoritative.

RECOMMENDATION CONCERNING MINIMUM AGE FOR ADMISSION TO EMPLOYMENT *

B

The General Conference of the International Labour Organisation,

Having been convened at Geneva by the Governing Body of the International Labour Office, and having met in its Fifty-eighth Session on 6 June 1973, and

Recognising that the effective abolition of child labour and the progressive raising of the minimum age for admission to employment constitute only one aspect of the protection and advancement of children and young persons, and

Noting the concern of the whole United Nations system with such protection and advancement, and

Having adopted the Minimum Age Convention, 1973, and

Desirous to define further certain elements of policy which are the concern of the International Labour Organisation, and

Having decided upon the adoption of certain proposals regarding minimum age for admission to employment, which is the fourth item on the agenda of the session, and

Having determined that these proposals shall take the form of a Recommendation supplementing the Minimum Age Convention, 1973,

adopts this twenty-sixth day of June of the year one thousand nine hundred and seventy-three the following Recommendation, which may be cited as the Minimum Age Recommendation, 1973 :

I. National policy

1. To ensure the success of the national policy provided for in Article 1 of the Minimum Age Convention, 1973, high priority should be given to planning for and meeting the needs of children and youth in national development policies and programmes and to the progressive extension of the inter-related measures necessary to provide the best possible conditions of physical and mental growth for children and young persons.

---

* Recommendation No. 146.

2. In this connection special attention should be given to such areas of planning and policy as the following :

(a) firm national commitment to full employment, in accordance with the Employment Policy Convention and Recommendation, 1964, and the taking of measures designed to promote employment-oriented development in rural and urban areas ;

(b) the progressive extension of other economic and social measures to alleviate poverty wherever it exists and to ensure family living standards and income which are such as to make it unnecessary to have recourse to the economic activity of children ;

(c) the development and progressive extension, without any discrimination, of social security and family welfare measures aimed at ensuring child maintenance, including children's allowances ;

(d) the development and progressive extension of adequate facilities for education and vocational orientation and training appropriate in form and content to the needs of the children and young persons concerned ;

(e) the development and progressive extension of appropriate facilities for the protection and welfare of children and young persons, including employed young persons, and for the promotion of their development.

3. Particular account should as necessary be taken of the needs of children and young persons who do not have families or do not live with their own families and of migrant children and young persons who live and travel with their families. Measures taken to that end should include the provision of fellowships and vocational training.

4. Full-time attendance at school or participation in approved vocational orientation or training programmes should be required and effectively ensured up to an age at least equal to that specified for admission to employment in accordance with Article 2 of the Minimum Age Convention, 1973.

5. (1) Consideration should be given to measures such as preparatory training, not involving hazards, for types of employment or work in respect of which the minimum age prescribed in accordance with Article 3 of the Minimum Age Convention, 1973, is higher than the age of completion of compulsory full-time schooling.

(2) Analogous measures should be envisaged where the professional exigencies of a particular occupation include a minimum age for admission which is higher than the age of completion of compulsory full-time schooling.

II. Minimum age

6. The minimum age should be fixed at the same level for all sectors of economic activity.

7. (1) Members should take as their objective the progressive raising to 16 years of the minimum age for admission to employment or work specified in pursuance of Article 2 of the Minimum Age Convention, 1973.

(2) Where the minimum age for employment or work covered by Article 2 of the Minimum Age Convention, 1973, is still below 15 years, urgent steps should be taken to raise it to that level.

8. Where it is not immediately feasible to fix a minimum age for all employment in agriculture and in related activities in rural areas, a minimum age should be fixed at least for employment on plantations and in the other agricultural

undertakings referred to in Article 5, paragraph 3, of the Minimum Age Convention, 1973.

III. Hazardous employment or work

9. Where the minimum age for admission to types of employment or work which are likely to jeopardise the health, safety or morals of young persons is still below 18 years, immediate steps should be taken to raise it to that level.

10. (1) In determining the types of employment or work to which Article 3 of the Minimum Age Convention, 1973, applies, full account should be taken of relevant international labour standards, such as those concerning dangerous substances, agents or processes (including ionising radiations), the lifting of heavy weights and underground work.

(2) The list of the types of employment or work in question should be re-examined periodically and revised as necessary, particularly in the light of advancing scientific and technological knowledge.

11. Where, by reference to Article 5 of the Minimum Age Convention, 1973, a minimum age is not immediately fixed for certain branches of economic activity or types of undertakings, appropriate minimum age provisions should be made applicable therein to types of employment or work presenting hazards for young persons.

IV. Conditions of employment

12. (1) Measures should be taken to ensure that the conditions in which children and young persons under the age of 18 years are employed or work reach and are maintained at a satisfactory standard. These conditions should be supervised closely.

(2) Measures should likewise be taken to safeguard and supervise the conditions in which children and young persons undergo vocational orientation and training within undertakings, training institutions and schools for vocational or technical education and to formulate standards for their protection and development.

13. (1) In connection with the application of the preceding Paragraph, as well as in giving effect to Article 7, paragraph 3, of the Minimum Age Convention, 1973, special attention should be given to—

(a) the provision of fair remuneration and its protection, bearing in mind the principle of equal pay for equal work ;

(b) the strict limitation of the hours spent at work in a day and in a week, and the prohibition of overtime, so as to allow enough time for education and training (including the time needed for homework related thereto), for rest during the day and for leisure activities ;

(c) the granting, without possibility of exception save in genuine emergency, of a minimum consecutive period of 12 hours' night rest, and of customary weekly rest days ;

(d) the granting of an annual holiday with pay of at least four weeks and, in any case, not shorter than that granted to adults ;

(e) coverage by social security schemes, including employment injury, medical care and sickness benefit schemes, whatever the conditions of employment or work may be ;

(f) the maintenance of satisfactory standards of safety and health and appropriate instruction and supervision.

(2) Subparagraph (1) of this Paragraph applies to young seafarers in so far as they are not covered in respect of the matters dealt with therein by international labour Conventions or Recommendations specifically concerned with maritime employment.

V. Enforcement

14. (1) Measures to ensure the effective application of the Minimum Age Convention, 1973, and of this Recommendation should include—

(a) the strengthening as necessary of labour inspection and related services, for instance by the special training of inspectors to detect abuses in the employment of work of children and young persons and to correct such abuses ; and

(b) the strengthening of services for the improvement and inspection of training in undertakings.

(2) Emphasis should be placed on the role which can be played by inspectors in supplying information and advice on effective means of complying with relevant provisions as well as in securing their enforcement.

(3) Labour inspection and inspection of training in undertakings should be closely co-ordinated to provide the greatest economic efficiency and, generally, the labour administration services should work in close co-operation with the services responsible for the education, training, welfare and guidance of children and young persons.

15. Special attention should be paid—

(a) to the enforcement of provisions concerning employment in hazardous types of employment or work ; and

(b) in so far as education or training is compulsory, to the prevention of the employment or work of children and young persons during the hours when instruction is available.

16. The following measures should be taken to facilitate the verification of ages :

(a) the public authorities should maintain an effective system of birth registration, which should include the issue of birth certificates ;

(b) employers should be required to keep and to make available to the competent authority registers or other documents indicating the names and ages or dates of birth, duly certified wherever possible, not only of children and young persons employed by them but also of those receiving vocational orientation or training in their undertakings ;

(c) children and young persons working in the streets, in outside stalls, in public places, in itinerant occupations or in other circumstances which make the checking of employers' records impracticable should be issued licences or other documents indicating their eligibility for such work.

INTERNATIONAL YEAR OF THE CHILD (1979) :
INFORMATION RECEIVED FROM GOVERNMENTS
OF MEMBER STATES ON ACTION IN RESPECT OF THE
MINIMUM AGE CONVENTION (NO. 138)
AND RECOMMENDATION (NO. 146), 1973 [1]

C

1. At its 204th Session (November 1977) the Governing Body of the International Labour Office considered that the ILO's contribution to the International Year of the Child should include a special effort to promote the implementation of the ILO's most recent comprehensive standards on the minimum age for admission to employment. It accordingly decided to invite the governments of member States :

(a) to consider taking such further action as might be necessary to give effect to the provisions of the Minimum Age Convention (No. 138) and Recommendation (No. 146), 1973, and to consider the ratification of the Convention, if not yet ratified ; and

(b) to inform the Director-General, by 31 July 1978, of any such action taken or contemplated and of any difficulties which in their view stand in the way of the implementation of the instruments in question and the ratification of the Convention.

The Governing Body requested the Director-General to submit to the Committee on Standing Orders and the Application of Conventions and Recommendations, in November 1978, a report summarising the information received, as a basis for consideration of any further action which might be called for at that stage.

2. The Governments of the following 58 States have supplied information : Argentina, Austria, Bahrain, Belgium, Bolivia, Brazil, Bulgaria, Burundi, Byelorussian SSR, Canada, Cuba, Cyprus, Czechoslovakia, Ethiopia, Finland, France, Gabon, German Democratic Republic, Federal Republic of Germany, Ghana, Guatemala, Hungary, India, Indonesia, Iran, Iraq, Ireland, Japan, Kenya, Libyan Arab Jamahiriya, Mali, Mauritius, Mexico, Morocco, New Zealand, Niger, Norway, Pakistan, Panama, Papua New Guinea, Paraguay, Philippines, Poland, Romania, Rwanda, Senegal, Spain, Sri Lanka, Suriname, Sweden, Switzerland, Tunisia, Ukrainian SSR, United Kingdom, Uruguay, Venezuela, Zaire, Zambia.

Ratification position and prospects with respect to Convention No. 138

3. Convention No. 138 has so far been ratified by the following 13 countries : Costa Rica, Cuba, Finland, Federal Republic of Germany, Ireland, Libyan Arab Jamahiriya, Luxembourg, Netherlands, Poland, Romania, Spain, Uruguay, Zambia.

4. In two countries—Bolivia and Iraq—the ratification of the Convention has been approved but not yet formally communicated to the ILO. The Government of Kenya proposes to ratify the Convention. In Burundi, Gabon, Italy and Zaire, a proposal for its ratification has been submitted to the legislature or the President. The Government of Tunisia, on the basis of a comparative study, has concluded that national legislation is in full conformity with the Convention ; its ratification is being examined. The Government of Czechoslovakia considers that national legislation is in conformity with Convention No. 138 and Recommendation No. 146 and, when certain minor points have been clarified, will examine the possibility of ratifying the Convention. Ratification is being considered in Rwanda. In Ghana, a recommendation in favour of ratification made by the tripartite Labour Advisory Committee is under consideration by the Government. The Governments of Mauritius and Norway have indicated that the implementation and ratification of the Convention are to be further considered by tripartite advisory bodies. The Government of the German Democratic Republic states that, on the occasion of the International Year of the Child, all ILO Conventions relating to the employment and training of children and young persons are being examined to decide whether they should be ratified or any other measures taken. In Cyprus a committee consisting of representatives of all the services concerned has been set up to consider the possibility of taking such action as may be necessary to give effect to Convention No. 138 and Recommendation No. 146.

5. The Government of the Byelorussian SSR states that its legislation and practice fully meet, and in many respects go beyond, the standards laid down in Convention No. 138. The Government of the Ukrainian SSR has provided particulars of legislation and practice corresponding to those given by the Byelorussian SSR.

6. The Government of the Federal Republic of Germany, which has ratified Convention No. 138, indicates that its legislation was amended to make the ratification possible. A number of governments which consider that their country is not at present in a position to ratify the Convention also refer to measures which have been taken or are contemplated to improve the protection in employment of children and young persons. The Government of India has adopted a National Policy for Children and established a National Children's Board for planning, review and co-ordination (of which the Prime Minister of India is president) ; the Government is committed to the gradual elimination of child labour, and measures to raise the minimum age in certain sectors are contemplated or in course of adoption. In the Philippines a "Decade of the Filipino Child 1977-87" has been declared and a National Plan of Action adopted. In Canada it is proposed to include consideration of the application of Convention No. 138 and Recommendation No. 146 in the agenda of the next federal-provincial meeting of Deputy Ministers of Labour. The Austrian Government has referred to the influence of Convention No. 138 on the raising of the minimum age for employment in agriculture and forestry. The Government of Suriname intends to raise the minimum age for employment of young persons as fishermen to 15 years, in conformity with Convention No. 112, and the Government of the United Kingdom is considering the adoption of regulations concerning minimum age for employment at sea which would make possible the ratification of Convention No. 58. Further particulars of measures contemplated are given below in the review of difficulties in the implementation of Convention No. 138 and Recommendation No. 146.

7. A number of governments, while providing some indications concerning their legislation on minimum age for employment, state that they are not in a position to ratify Convention No. 138. Many of them consider it difficult, at their country's present stage of development, to extend minimum age protection to all

sectors of activity, to raise the minimum age to the required level, or to ensure general observance of minimum age standards. Problems of this kind are mentioned by the Governments of Argentina, Brazil, Ethiopia, India, Indonesia, Iran, Mali, Mexico, Morocco, Pakistan, Papua New Guinea, Paraguay, Sri Lanka, Suriname and Venezuela. It is not apparent from the replies whether, in all these cases, full account has been taken of the range of flexibility permitted by the Convention as regards the sectors to be covered by minimum age provisions, the possibility of excluding limited categories of employment, the fixing of the general minimum age at 14 years (instead of 15 years) in the case of developing countries, and the authorisation of employment in light work as from the age of 13 years (or 12 years, for countries fixing the general minimum age at 14 years). More specific difficulties mentioned by governments are analysed below.

Difficulties in the implementation of Convention No. 138

Scope

8. The Convention, in contrast to earlier minimum age Conventions applicable to limited economic sectors (which it is designed gradually to replace), applies to all forms of employment or work. However, a State whose economy and administrative facilities are insufficiently developed may initially limit the scope of application of the Convention, but must apply it at least to mining and quarrying ; manufacturing ; construction ; electricity, gas and water ; sanitary services ; transport, storage and communication ; and plantations and other agricultural undertakings mainly producing for commercial purposes, but excluding family and small-scale holdings producing for local consumption and not regularly employing hired workers. In addition, limited categories of employment or work in respect of which special and substantial problems of application arise may be excluded, provided that they do not involve danger to health, safety or morals.

9. The Government of Canada indicates that, although school attendance is compulsory everywhere at least up to 15 years, it remains necessary to establish a minimum age for employment in agriculture ; in addition, in two jurisdictions no minimum age exists for work in factories, hotels and restaurants. In Norway and Switzerland minimum age provisions do not at present apply to agriculture ; in the former country it is proposed to extend them to that sector. In India minimum age legislation does not cover all activities to which the Convention must be applied even under the special relaxation for developing countries. In Pakistan minimum age provisions do not apply in agriculture and the rural industrial sector. The reply from the Government of Bahrain mentions only legislation applicable to the private sector.

10. The Governments of Sweden and Switzerland indicate that the existing minimum age legislation applies only to persons working under an employment relationship, whereas the Convention is not confined to such persons.

Minimum age

11. The Convention requires ratifying States to specify a minimum age which should not be less than the age of completion of compulsory schooling, and in any case not less than 15 years. A country whose economy and educational facilities are insufficiently developed may, however, initially specify a minimum age of 14 years. Of the 13 countries which have so far ratified the Convention, all but two have specified a minimum age of 15 years ; the Libyan Arab Jamahiriya and Romania specified 18 and 16 years respectively. Most of the non-ratifying States

which have supplied information on their legislation appear to have set their general minimum age at a level consistent with the minimum standard of 15 years (or 14 years permitted initially for developing countries) laid down in the Convention.

12. The Belgian Government states that the only obstacle to ratification of the Convention is the fact that compulsory schooling ends at 14 years, whereas the Convention fixes a minimum age for employment of 15 years ; the extension of compulsory schooling is contemplated. In Hungary compulsory schooling covers eight classes, which most children complete by the age of 14 ; however, more than 90 per cent continue their studies. The Government considers that it would be inappropriate to deprive the small number who do not continue their studies after the age of 14 of the possibility of entering employment, and refers to special conditions applicable to workers under 16 years (reduced hours, additional paid leave, prohibition of night work and of employment in arduous or unhealthy work). In Switzerland, in cantons where the school-leaving age is 14 years children who have completed their schooling may be employed, without limitation of such employment to light work. The Austrian Government mentions that, while in general children complete their compulsory education and can take up work only after they have reached the age of 15 years, exceptionally compulsory education may be completed and employment taken for a brief period before that age. The Canadian Government states that in one province with a school-leaving age of 16 years the minimum age for employment is 15.

13. A number of developing countries indicate that their legislation does not yet meet the 14-year minimum age standard which Convention No. 138 would permit them to apply initially. In Indonesia, Iran and Morocco the general minimum age for entry into employment is 12 years. The Government of Iran states that draft amending legislation now under consideration would raise this age to 14 years. The Government of Indonesia is examining the possibility of similar action. In Morocco a draft Labour Code would provide for a minimum age of 13 years. In India, while a minimum age of 14 or 15 years is laid down for employment in a wide range of industrial activities, rail and motor transport, merchant shipping, etc., the minimum age for work on plantations is 12 years and for employment in shops and commercial establishments it varies from 12 to 14 years (but was recently raised to 15 in one state). The raising of the minimum age under the Plantations Act to 14 years is to be examined when that Act is next amended, and state governments have been requested to raise the minimum age for shops and commercial establishments to 14 years, where this is not already the case ; some state governments have already agreed to take such action. The Government of Pakistan reports that the minimum age under the Factories Act and the legislation on shops and commercial establishments was recently raised from 12 to 14 years. In Argentina children under 14 years may be permitted to work when this is necessary for their own or their family's subsistence. The Government of Venezuela states that, although the minimum age for employment is 14 years, economic factors frequently lead children to take up work before that age, and it considers that it would be justified to lower the minimum age to 13 years in such cases provided that it is limited to light work as permitted by the Convention.

14. In general, where the minimum age standard provided for in the Convention cannot yet be fully attained, it would seem appropriate to re-examine the legislation with due regard to the provisions of the Convention relating to light work. In some cases the possibility of excluding limited categories of employment or work from the application of the Convention may also make it possible to overcome marginal problems.

Dangerous work

15. The Convention provides that the minimum age for admission to employment or work dangerous to health, safety or morals shall be not less than 18 years or, under certain conditions, 16 years. It leaves the employments in question to be determined by each State after consultation with employers' and workers' organisations.

16. From the information supplied it would appear that the principle of setting the level for admission to dangerous work at 18 years is widely accepted, although the range of jobs to which that standard applies varies considerably. The Government of Canada, however, indicates that in general Canadian legislation does not contain a definition of "dangerous employment" and that, while the minimum age for underground work in mines is generally 18 years, it is 17 years in one province and the federal jurisdiction. In Mexico and Morocco the minimum age for dangerous work is in general 16 years. In Austria, for agriculture and forestry, there exists no list of employments prohibited for persons under 18 years. In France the application to employment in agriculture of the general provisions on dangerous work prohibited for young persons is dependent on the issue of a decree now under consideration. In Norway, where a number of specific prohibitions of employment in dangerous work of persons under 18 years are contained in the basic legislation, detailed regulations to supplement these provisions are being prepared. In Sweden measures to meet the requirements of Convention No. 138 as regards dangerous work on board ship are under consideration.

Light work

17. The Convention leaves it open to ratifying States to permit the employment on light work which is not harmful to their health or development, and not prejudicial to attendance at school or participation in vocational orientation or training programmes, of children between 13 and 15 years (or between 12 and 14 years for States having specified a general minimum age of 14 years) and of children above that age who are still subject to compulsory schooling. From the information supplied it appears that most countries permit the employment on light work of children below the general minimum age. However, in several countries where the general minimum age is 15 (Austria, Japan) or 16 (France) light work is permitted as from the age of 12, instead of 13 as specified in the Convention. The Government of Sweden indicates that, while light work is permitted only in limited circumstances, there is no lower age limit for such work. The Government of New Zealand indicates that children may be employed part-time on certain forms of light work, the prohibition of which would not have public support or appear necessary. The Government of Mauritius mentions the possibility for children under 15 to be employed in light work in agriculture and the construction industry, without indicating whether this is subject to any minimum age condition.

18. The Convention also permits exceptions from minimum age standards to be made, by permits granted in individual cases, for such purposes as participation in artistic performances. The United Kingdom Government states that its legislation allows children to take part without permit in such performances subject to defined conditions, observance of which is subject to inspection and enforced by penal sanctions. The Government considers that the welfare of the children is safeguarded and does not propose to alter the legislation.

Consultation

19. The Convention provides for the consultation of the employers' and workers' organisations concerned on various matters such as the determination

of dangerous occupations and certain exclusions or exceptions. The Government of Brazil states that, while national legislation already contains provisions on child labour corresponding to those of the Convention, with due regard to conditions obtaining in developing countries, the system does not permit the consultation of employers' and workers' organisations in the form required by the Convention.

Enforcement

20. The Convention contains various provisions relating to the enforcement of its provisions, including the provision of appropriate penalties and the keeping of registers or other documents by employers. The United Kingdom Government indicates that its legislation requires the keeping of registers only in industrial employment and that the standard of record-keeping is poor especially among small employers. However, legislation on non-industrial employment of school children is being reviewed, and the making of regulations to require employers to keep records of children employed is contemplated. The Governments of several other countries (Indonesia, Mali, Pakistan, Venezuela) refer more generally to the difficulties encountered in enforcing existing minimum age legislation in view of prevailing economic conditions.

Comments regarding the implementation of Recommendation No. 146

21. Only relatively few replies refer specifically to the situation with regard to Recommendation No. 146. The Governments of Ireland and Norway state that they have accepted this Recommendation. The Government of Sweden states that the aspirations expressed in the Recommendation are in general agreement with Swedish attitudes (although national legislation prescribes a night rest of 11 hours for young persons, as compared with the 12-hour rest provided for in the Recommendation). The Government of India, while giving particulars of its national policy to promote the welfare of children and of its efforts to raise the minimum age for employment, states that the objective of the progressive raising of the minimum age to 16 years stated in the Recommendation is not easy of attainment in developing countries like India. The Government of Kenya also states that it cannot at present ensure full-time education or training of all children under 16 years. The Governments of the Byelorussian SSR, Czechoslovakia, France, Norway, Romania, the Ukrainian SSR and the United Kingdom indicate that the general minimum age for employment in their countries is 16 years ; in Spain the minimum age is being raised to this level in conjunction with the introduction of new educational and training measures. The Government of Japan considers that the raising of the minimum age from 15 to 16 years requires careful study, including its relation to the completion of compulsory education. It also mentions that national legislation does not ensure a night rest of 12 hours for young persons nor entitle them to a special annual holiday with pay. The Governments of Austria and the United Kingdom refer to the difficulties mentioned in connection with the Convention. The latter Government also states that it cannot accept responsibility for application of certain provisions of the Recommendation relating to matters (hours of work, night rest, holidays with pay) which are normally dealt with by collective bargaining.

Conclusions

22. The information available indicates that the general principles underlying Convention No. 138 and Recommendation No. 146 find a very wide measure of support and that the problem of child labour is receiving close

attention from national policy makers, both within the framework of the International Year of the Child and as an important aspect of economic and social development planning. In many countries measures to improve the protection of children and young persons in regard to work have recently been taken or are under consideration. It would appear that Convention No. 138 and Recommendation No. 146, as a comprehensive and up-to-date statement of internationally agreed principles, are providing a direct source of inspiration and reference in this process. Their use in this connection is facilitated by the dynamic but flexible approach adopted in these instruments : they aim at a progressive raising of standards ; they permit the gradual integration of young persons into active life on the basis of distinctions between light work, employment in general and dangerous occupations ; and they make allowance for the varying possibilities of countries at different stages of development.

23. Nevertheless, the information so far available does not permit of a full or precise analysis of the situation with regard to the implementation of Convention No. 138 and Recommendation No. 146. Less than half the member States have provided information. The replies received vary considerably in volume and detail, and frequently they do not clearly identify the problems which may impede acceptance of these standards. In particular, while a number of developing countries express doubt as to their ability to ratify Convention No. 138, many of them do not provide any detailed analysis of the difficulties encountered or seek to accommodate these difficulties within the different flexibility devices embodied in the Convention. A more detailed examination of these questions would be useful, bearing in mind the relationship between the raising of minimum age standards and other aspects of social policy to which reference is made in Recommendation No. 146 (such as measures to combat youth unemployment and to develop and adapt facilities for education and training). Furthermore, it has not been possible within the present context to analyse ways in which the various difficulties mentioned by governments might be resolved. This aspect also would merit further review.

24. To permit fuller study of national law and practice regarding the minimum age for admission to employment and to facilitate the application of the Convention and Recommendation of 1973, it would appear useful to obtain reports from member States under the provisions of article 19 of the Constitution (reports on unratified Conventions and Recommendations). This would provide a basis for a general survey of the situation by the Committee of Experts on the Application of Conventions and Recommendations. A proposal that Convention No. 138 and Recommendation No. 146 should be chosen for reports under this procedure in 1980 is made in another paper presented to the Committee. [2] The Committee, in considering that proposal, will no doubt wish to take into account the information and comments contained in the present paper.

Geneva, 1 Nov. 1978.

Notes

[1] This appendix reproduces doc. GB.208/SC/I/6 of the Committee on Standing Orders and the Application of Conventions and Recommendations of the Governing Body of the ILO.

[2] At its 208th Session (November 1978) the Governing Body decided to request governments to submit reports under article 19 of the Constitution in 1980 on the Minimum Age Convention, 1973 (No. 138), and Recommendation, 1973 (No. 146).

DECLARATION BY THE DIRECTOR-GENERAL OF THE ILO CONCERNING THE INTERNATIONAL YEAR OF THE CHILD *

D

Resolution 31/169 adopted by the General Assembly on 21 December 1976 proclaimed 1979 the International Year of the Child, with the general objectives of promoting the well-being of children, drawing attention to their special needs and encouraging national action on behalf of children, particularly for the least privileged and those who are at work.

This International Year is of special importance to the ILO, which, even since its foundation in 1919, has sought to restrict child labour and provide protection for children. In doing so, the ILO has acted in accordance with the principle set forth in the United Nations Declaration of the Rights of the Child—that a child has a right to protection against exploitation. Despite the efforts made by the ILO and by many countries which have laid down regulations on the minimum age for admission of children to employment and on the conditions of employment of children, child labour is still widespread and a disturbing problem in many parts of the world where poverty and tradition have precluded its elimination.

In the light of ILO standards, the International Year should enable governments and employers' and workers' organisations the world over to assess the situation of children at work and also give the competent national bodies and the ILO an opportunity and the means to strengthen their action programmes for children. For that purpose the ILO urgently appeals to them to apply its standards on the minimum age for admission to employment and the conditions of employment of children. Action should be based on the following principles : *(a)* a child is not a "small adult" but a person entitled to self-fulfilment through learning and play so that his adult life is not jeopardised by his having had to work at an early age ; *(b)* governments should, in co-operation with all the national organisations concerned, take all necessary social and legislative action for the progressive elimination of child labour ; *(c)* pending the elimination of child labour, it must be regulated and humanised.

I therefore declare the ILO's endorsement of the aims of the International Year of the Child and its pledge to make every effort and lend all support to member States for their earliest possible fulfilment.

---

* Declaration endorsed by the ILO Governing Body at its 209th Session, February-March 1979.

RESOLUTION CONCERNING THE INTERNATIONAL YEAR OF THE CHILD AND THE PROGRESSIVE ELIMINATION OF CHILD LABOUR AND TRANSITIONAL MEASURES *

E

The General Conference of the International Labour Organisation,

Recalling resolution 31/169 adopted by the United Nations General Assembly, proclaiming 1979 as the International Year of the Child, with the general objectives of promoting the well-being of children, drawing attention to their special needs and encouraging national action on behalf of children, particularly for the least privileged and those who are at work,

Noting the activities that were undertaken at the national, regional and international levels in preparation for the International Year of the Child and the progress made since,

Convinced that the International Year of the Child provides for all member States an opportunity to review their economic and social policies concerning child welfare and to formulate guidelines in this sphere,

Considering that a new and fair international economic order would greatly contribute towards genuine economic and social development, primarily of benefit to children,

Recalling the endorsement by the ILO of the aims of the International Year of the Child and its pledge to make every effort and lend all support to member States for their earliest possible fulfilment,

Recalling the United Nations Declaration of the Rights of the Child, 1959, and particularly Principle 9, which stipulates that the child should be protected against all forms of neglect, cruelty and exploitation ; that he should not be admitted to employment before an appropriate minimum age ; and that he should in no case be caused or permitted to engage in any occupation or employment which would prejudice his health or education, or interfere with his physical, mental or moral development,

Considering that since its foundation the International Labour Organisation has sought to eliminate child labour and to provide protection of children,

Noting with approval the Director-General's Declaration on the International Year of the Child,

Deeply concerned that child labour still remains widespread in many parts of the world and that working children frequently work under conditions including those of exploitation detrimental to their health and welfare,

---

* Adopted by the International Labour Conference at its 65th Session in June 1979.

Recognising the need to ensure that the health and strength and the tender age of children are not abused and that children are not permitted to enter avocations unsuited to their age or strength,

Considering that the International Year of the Child should be an occasion to reaffirm with practical measures and deeds that the well-being of today's children is the concern of all people everywhere,

Recalling the decision of the Governing Body of the International Labour Office, taken at its 208th Session (November 1978), to request the member States to supply a report in 1980 under article 19 of the Constitution on the extent to which effect has been given or is proposed to be given to the Minimum Age Convention (No. 138) and Recommendation (No. 146) of 1973 :

1. Calls upon member States to strengthen their efforts for the elimination of child labour and for the protection of children, and in this context—

(a) to implement the provisions of the Minimum Age Convention, 1973 (No. 138), and, where they have not already done so, to ratify this Convention as early as practicable ;

(b) to ensure in particular full recognition of the principle that any work undertaken by children who have not completed their compulsory education shall not be such as would prejudice their education or development ;

(c) to apply the Minimum Age Recommendation, 1973 (No. 146), and the Minimum Age (Underground Work) Recommendation, 1965 (No. 124) ;

(d) to report in detail in 1980 under the procedure of article 19 of the Constitution on the progress reached in the implementation of the Minimum Age Convention (No. 138) and Recommendation (No. 146), 1973 ;

(e) pending the elimination of child labour, to take all necessary social and legislative action for the progressive elimination of child labour and, during the transitional period until the elimination of child labour, to regulate and humanise it and to give particular attention to the implementation of special standards for children relating to medical examination, night work, underground work, working hours, weekly rest, paid annual leave and certain types of hazardous and dangerous work embodied in a number of ILO instruments ;

(f) to make every effort to extend the provisions of appropriate educational facilities, in order fully to apply compulsory education and to introduce it where it does not exist and, where education is compulsory, to make it effective ;

(g) to ensure that appropriate protective labour legislation applies to all children at work in the sectors of activity in which they are employed ;

(h) to ensure that special attention is given to the provision of fair remuneration and to its protection for the benefit of the child ;

(i) to strengthen, where appropriate, labour inspection and to undertake all other measures conducive to the elimination of child labour ;

(j) (i) to identify the special needs of children, to strengthen efforts to improve the general economic and social well-being of the family, and to launch a national campaign aimed at creating awareness among the general public of the adverse effects of child labour on his/her development ;

(ii) to develop international solidarity and co-operation with the developing countries and to activate efforts to establish a new and fair international economic order so as to respond more effectively to the basic measures undertaken by each State for better child protection.

2 Calls upon governments and employers' and workers' organisations to assess the situation of child work and to assist the competent bodies and the ILO to strengthen their action programme for children.

3. Invites the Governing Body of the International Labour Office to instruct the Director-General to continue and reinforce the ILO's action through such means as factual surveys of national situations and practices for the elimination of child labour and for the protection of children at work, and to make the necessary preparations for a global revision of the relevant ILO instruments.

NOTES ON THE PHOTOGRAPHS

F

Facing p. 14—Children and young people frequently act as assistants to adult workers in a very wide range of jobs, especially in the developing countries. This young plasterer's mate, like so many youngsters of his age, is doing work that is both heavy and dirty. (*Photo :* © CIRIC, Geneva)

Facing p. 15—(*Above*) The street shoeblack is a familiar figure in many Third World cities. His income is irregular and inadequate, like that of his family as a whole and of the world to which he belongs. (*Photo :* ILO)
(*Below*) In the hope that some passer-by will sooner or later buy their wares, countless children in the developing countries waste their childhood years at the roadside, far removed from the classroom and with no chance of playing with other children. (*Photo :* J.-P. Laffont, SYGMA)

Facing p. 30—Children of both sexes are excessively exploited in many factories and workshops, particularly in clandestine undertakings in the informal sector. Such cases are rarely discovered by the understaffed labour inspection services ; when they are, they usually lead to an outcry in the local newspapers and periodicals. (*Photo :* ILO)

Facing p. 31—(*Above*) In general, the small factories and workshops of the informal sector are those with the worst conditions of work, safety and hygiene. The child worker, who is generally set to work by his parents to keep him from vagrancy, is forced to labour under these conditions and is unable to attend school (at any rate, not full-time) or to take healthy recreation (where facilities exist). (*Photo :* ILO)
(*Below*) In many Third World countries children from impoverished families spend long hours of the day—and sometimes the night—selling goods on the public highway. Such children run the risk of injury from passing vehicles and, moreover, are in constant moral danger. (*Photo :* X)

Facing p. 78—In a good number of countries stretching in a broad arc from north-west Africa to southern Asia, girls are traditionally introduced to the hand carpet-manufacturing industry at a very early age. With their slender fingers they can tie the small, tight knots that increase a carpet's value. They form a docile and cheap labour force. (*Photo :* J.-P. Laffont, SYGMA)

Facing p. 79—Poverty forces children to accept strenuous and unpleasant jobs. The load that this young rubbish-collector is carrying is too heavy for his immature body to bear without strain. The harmful effects of such jobs on physical growth are undeniable. (*Photo :* J.-P. Laffont, SYGMA)

Children at work

Facing p. 94—*(Above)* In some countries very young children have been found working in the brick-making industry. (*Photo :* J.-P. Laffont, SYGMA)
(Below) In the more economically advanced countries the exploitation of children belongs to the past. Regrettably, this is not so in many countries of the Third World. This photograph, taken in 1978, shows two children working in a coal mine. (*Photo :* J.-P. Laffont, SYGMA)

Facing p. 95—In very poor households, living conditions rarely reach the basic minimum standards. A great many children in such households, if they are not directly engaged in production work, have to undertake (at far too early an age) those domestic tasks which a mother forced by poverty to obtain a job outside the home cannot do. (*Photo :* J.-P. Laffont, SYGMA)

Facing p. 110—It is common knowledge that most working children in both the developed and the developing countries are employed in agriculture, above all in family undertakings. Sometimes they just do light work, but in many cases they perform the same tasks as the adults. Most of those children are beyond the reach of the labour inspection services. (*Photo :* J.-P. Laffont, SYGMA)

Facing p. 111—*(Above)* These young stone-hewers belong to the world of "small adults" : they neither learn nor play enough but expend their physical and mental energy on jobs that they should not be doing ; they grow up in an unhealthy environment ; and at the same time mortgage their whole future. Such a life is abnormal for young people of their age. (*Photo :* J.-P. Laffont, SYGMA)
(Below) The concentration that is needed to operate a machine, the fact that machines are designed for adults rather than for children and, often, the lack of adequate guards and other protective devices are all factors that greatly increase a child worker's fatigue, with all its consequences—in particular, the risk of occupational accidents. (*Photo :* X)

Facing p. 126—*(Above)* In many countries boys are employed on craftwork in the ceramics, leather, wood, metal and other industries. (*Photo :* J.-P. Laffont, SYGMA)
(Below) Working children are more exposed to occupational hazards than adult workers doing the same kind of job. This is partly due to the lack of concentration that is characteristic of childhood. These itinerant petrol-sellers are being treated in hospital for burns received during their work. (*Photo :* J.-P. Laffont, SYGMA)

Facing p. 127—Many children in developing countries, like this small African child, are "hired out" or "handed over" by their parents, who are unable to meet even the most basic of their needs. (*Photo :* J.-P, Laffont, SYGMA)

GUIDE TO FURTHER READING

G

Publications of the International Labour Office (ILO)

Conditions of work of women and young workers on plantations, Report III, Committee on Work on Plantations, Sixth Session, Geneva, 1970.

Minimum age for admission to employment, Report (IV) 1, International Labour Conference, 57th Session, Geneva, 1972.

Population and labour (Geneva, 1973).

Porter, Robin : "Child labour in Hong Kong and related problems : A brief review", in *International Labour Review* (Geneva), May 1975.

Report on the ILO/SIDA Asian Regional Seminar on Labour Inspection in Relation to the Employment of Women and Protection of Children (Singapore, 28 November-13 December 1972) (Geneva, 1973).

Publications of the United Nations

Children and adolescents in slums and shanty-towns in developing countries (New York, Economic and Social Council, docs. E/ICEF/L.1277 and E/ICEF/L./1277/Add.1, 5 Mar. 1971 ; mimeographed).

A handbook for family and child welfare (New York, 1971 ; Sales No. : 69.IV.1).

Report on children (New York, 1971 ; Sales No. : 71.IV.3).

Publications of the United Nations Children's Fund (UNICEF)

Assignment Children : A Journal concerned with Children, Women and Youth in Development (Geneva), two double issues per year.

Children of the developing countries : A report by UNICEF (Cleveland and New York, World Publishing Co., 1963).

Drumel, J. ; Voisin, M. : *L'enfant, cette personne* (Brussels, Elsevier Sequoia, 1979).

Other publications

Associazione Cristiane Lavoratori Italiani (ACLI) : *Libro bianco sul lavoro minorile* (Rome, 1967).

Clopper, E. N. : *Child labor in city streets* (New York, Garrett Press, 1970).

Costin, Lela B. : *Child welfare : Policies and practice* (New York, McGraw-Hill, 1972).

Johnson, S. : *The population problem* (Newton Abbot, David and Charles, 1973).

E. de H. Lobo : *Children of immigrants to Britain : Their health and social problems* (London, Hodder and Stoughton, 1978).

Singh, M. ; Kaura, V. D. ; Khan, S. A. : *Working children in Bombay : A study* (New Delhi, National Institute of Public Co-operation and Child Development, 1978).

"Work out of school : The Emrys Davies Report", in *Education* (London), 10 Nov. 1972.